Research Centre for the History of Religious and Cultural Diversity
(Meiji University, Tokyo)

Memory and Narrative Series Two 1

The Life Story of Mr Ram Krishan (Prashar)
A Hindu in Coventry from Punjab, India

Edited and written by Kiyotaka Sato

With support from Eleanor Nesbitt

Foreword by Pippa Virdee

The memory and narrative series is published by Kiyotaka Sato, Professor of European History, School of Arts and Letters, Meiji University, Tokyo. The purpose of the project is to enable the UK's many and various ethnic minority communities and indigenous groups to record and preserve their memories, life experiences and traditions, and to ensure access to this rich inheritance for present and future generations. The project is established with financial support from Meiji University as well as the Ministry of Education, Culture, Sports, Science and Technology (Japan) and other organisations.

First published by RCHRCD, December 2016

Copyright © 2016 Kiyotaka Sato

Research Centre for the History of Religious and Cultural Diversity (RCHRCD)
Meiji University, Tokyo
1-1 Kandasurugadai, Chiyoda-ku,
Tokyo, 101-8301, Japan
Email: satokiyo@meiji.ac.jp

All rights reserved. No part of this publication may be reproduced, stored in a retrieval system, or transmitted in any form, or by any means, electronic, mechanical, photocopying, recording or otherwise, without the prior permission in writing of the author. Enquiries concerning reproduction outside these terms and in other countries should be sent to the editor at the address above.

Outside front cover:
  Mr Ram Krishan
  (Reproduced with the permission of Mr Ram Krishan; photography by Ania Bas)
Inside front cover:
  Mr Ram Krishan
  (Reproduced with the permission of Mr Ram Krishan; photography by Michael Youett)
Outside back cover:
  Mr Ram Krishan and his wife Eleanor Nesbitt
  (Reproduced with the permission of Mr Ram Krishan)

ISSN 2185-6079

Published Asia Printing Office Corporation
Address: 1154 Miwa araya, Nagano-shi, Nagano, 380-0804, Japan

Acknowledgements

I wish to thank the following people and organisations who assisted me with my work:

Mrs Delia Baker
Professor Emeritus Richard Bonney, University of Leicester
Mrs Cynthia Brown (former Project Manager of the East Midlands Oral History Archive [EMOHA], University of Leicester)
Mrs Yoshimi Gregory (Chair, Leicestershire Japan Society)
Ms Elizabeth Wayne Hawker (Head of Religious Education, Soar Valley College, Leicester)
Associate Professor Jenny Holt, Meiji University
Mr Colin Hyde (Researcher and outreach officer of the East Midlands Oral History Archive [EMOHA], University of Leicester)
Mr Shuichi Kurosaki (part-time lecturer, Meiji University)
Professor Eleanor Nesbitt, Emeritus Professor of Religions and Education, University of Warwick
Mrs Hideko Okamoto (Chair, Hiroshima Coventry Club)
Professor Toru Okamoto, Hiroshima Shudo University
Mr Keith Perry (Editor, The Coventry Telegraph)
Mrs Sonia Spencer
Dr Pippa Virdee, Senior Lecturer, De Montfort University

De Montfort University, Leicester
Coventry City Council
The Hindu Temple Society (Coventry)
Coventry Multi-Faith Forum
University of Leicester
University of Warwick

Above all I wish to thank Mr Ram Krishan both for the interviews he gave in preparation for this booklet, and for all the other information he has given me regarding his life story.

Foreword

The life story of Ram Krishan is the first publication in the second series of Memory and Narrative by Professor Sato. He has worked tirelessly in recent years to compile the life stories of individuals who have contributed to making Britain rich, vibrant and diverse. This is particularly poignant as I write this on the eve of the UK referendum on whether or not we remain in the EU. Through Ram's life story we can travel through colonial India to a country in jubilation and broken at the same time during the Partition of Punjab and independence in 1947. By the 1950s we are transported to post-war Britain, a country recovering from the effects of World War Two, and through Ram's experiences we can witness the immense change in British society to now, when Europe is in many ways at another pivotal cross-junction.

Ram Krishan, born in 1931, came to Britain in 1954 from Nawanshahr in Punjab, India. The name Nawanshahr literally translates into 'new city' and it is located not far from what is undoubtedly the artery of north India, the Grand Trunk Road that connected Kabul to Calcutta in Mughal India. It is an area linked with many transient (and eventually permanent) invaders and has a long tradition of out-migration too. Many of the early Punjabis that settled in post-war Britain came from this region. But Ram Krishan's account and early life are firmly embedded in the late colonial history of the British in India. His early experiences and encounters are from colonial Calcutta where his father worked for a Marwari (see no. 3, page 60) firm and then later in Punjab, which witnessed the worst of the Partition violence. Interestingly, both Bengal (where Calcutta is located) and Punjab bore the brunt of independence when these two provinces were divided to form Pakistan.

Born into a Hindu Brahmin family, Ram Krishan from a young age was exposed to religious learning through his home life and his father in Calcutta. Annual trips to visit his grandparents in Nawanshahr would include a long train journey that included stops at prominent religious sites such as Ayodhya, Benares (Banaras), and Mathura. Yet what stands out in Ram's account of his early life is the multiplicity of the different religious influences, both in Calcutta and Nawanshahr, where he eventually moved in 1941 in response to Japanese incursions at the eastern border of India. From his early childhood accounts of going to the Satyanarayan Temple and Kali Ghat to influences from his maternal family's association with Kartarpur and accounts of Sikh mythology, the influences of the Goddess Durga and the local *pir* [Muslim holy man] and historical and familial links with Sikhism are all brought together seamlessly and without tension between them. This is important because of the stronger sense of a distinct identity and its boundaries which exist today in all of these religions. In his story it is clear that Ram was very much influenced by his father who he describes as a "thinking liberal" and the pluralistic and open nature of Punjabi society. This, along with his academic interests in Hindi and Sanskrit, led to long lasting emotional relationship with both literature and religion.

An avid interest in politics started in Calcutta, with exposure to the nationalist movement through his father's support for the Indian National Congress, including a fascinating account of his father's encounter with Gandhi. Ram Krishan's relationship with political activism remained with him even after he migrated to Coventry – initially with the Indian Workers' Association, but then developing this into a more cultural and social activism to support the community that had settled in the UK. Later on in life he contributed actively to the promotion and growth of the Hindu Temple Society in Coventry. Undoubtedly the most glamorous of his involvements was in establishing the Indian Cultural and Welfare Society in 1958. It had a dual role of both providing entertainment and alongside this was the more cultural and social welfare. The latter included writing letters on behalf of people that Ram worked with in the foundries or others who were not literate and wanted to send letters back home. One is immediately reminded of the 2008 Hindi film by Shyam Benegal, *Welcome to Sajjanpur*. In the film the main protagonist is an unemployed graduate who ends up writing letters on behalf of the colourful and endearing fellow villagers. And in the late 50s and early 60s Ram himself had the opportunity to host prominent Indian actors and actresses to Coventry, alongside regular film screenings; this sort of exposure and familial contact with "stars" would be impossible in today's world. The activities themselves allow us to venture into the little known social and cultural scene of early migrants to Coventry who often had limited forms of entertainment available to them. The colour bar ensured segregation and going to the General Wolfe pub in Coventry was fine if you drank and were a man, but there were few other options open to friends and families to get together.

These are only some of the glimpses into the life of Ram Krishan; the full story moves from city to city, from India to Britain, to the challenges and anxieties of settling down in a new country. Like many of his friends Ram came to Britain to work and was driven by a sense of adventure with little thought to settling down and making Coventry his permanent home. Throughout all of this adventure, the narrative provided by Ram and recorded by Professor Sato transports the reader back in time, whether this is colonial Calcutta or the small town of Nawanshahr, or then arriving in the booming city of Coventry in the 1950s. The smells, the weather, the people and the places are all beautifully narrated here and offer a wonderful glimpse of social cultural history. Ram lived in Calcutta when World War II was declared on behalf of India; as the war came closer the family shifted back to their ancestral home – only then to witness the great Partition in 1947 and the extraordinary ways in which it transformed the region. Yet when Ram arrived in Coventry, he probably had little idea that this was a city ravaged by that same war and that he would now contribute to rebuilding it. The ebbs and flows of people in the past sixty years had defined and re-defined not just Britain but towns and cities across the modern world. This account offers us a life story of Ram and his family with the backdrop of pivotal moments in history.

Dr Pippa Virdee
Coventry
17 June 2016

Mr Ram Krishan

At St Pancras International Station in London in 2013. I am standing beside the statue of poet Sir John Betjeman who saved the station from demolition.

CONTENTS

Acknowledgements	5
Foreword	6
I. Introduction	11
II. The Life Story of Mr Ram Krishan (Prashar)	19
1 Life in Kolkata (Calcutta) and my primary education	20
2 Life in Nawanshahr: my family and my secondary education	26
3 World War II (1939-1945) and the Partition of India in 1947	32
4 My higher education and departure to England in 1954	36
5 New life in Coventry: work and leisure, illness, discrimination	41
6 The Indian Workers' Association (IWA) and the Indian Cultural and Welfare Society (ICWS)	47
7 Getting married	49
8 Community organisations and interfaith relations in Coventry	53
9 Japan and Japanese culture	58
10 Changing my passport	59
III. Eleanor's contribution to Ram's story	71
IV. Appendices	79
Appendix 1: Photo memories of Mr Ram Krishan and his family	80
Appendix 2: The Indian Cultural and Welfare Society (ICWS)	95
Appendix 3: The Hindu Temple Society (Coventry)	99
Appendix 4: Coventry Multi-Faith Forum	108
Appendix 5: Other activities of Mr Ram Krishan	118

Appendix 6: Ethnicity and religion in the UK and Coventry	132
Appendix 7: Maps of the Punjab region (India) and of Coventry in the UK	134
Appendix 8: Select bibliography and websites	139
Appendix 9: A message from Mr Ram Krishan	144

I
Introduction

I   Introduction

First of all, I would like to explain why I have embarked on publishing a second series of *Memory and Narrative* biographies, in addition to the nine booklets which constitute series one.[1] The main purpose for compiling this series is the same as my purpose (see the inside front cover) in publishing the original series. However, series two differs from the first series in two respects. The first is that while the original series focussed on people living in Leicester or with strong links with Leicester, the new series includes individuals from outside Leicester. Eventually, it may evolve to include people not only from various parts of Britain, but also from other parts of the world. At present, only the contents of the first booklet have been finished. My future research will determine where the settings for the subsequent narratives will be.

The second difference between series one and series two is that, even when series two features people who live in Leicester or who have strong links with that city, when I wish to edit it freely in a very different way from the remit for series one, I will use series two to achieve this. Therefore, I hope that series two will, like the discussion papers[2] published to accompany series one, fill various gaps that exist in the first series. I hope series two will be greeted as warmly by readers as series one.

This publication, number one in the second series, focuses on the life story of Mr Ram Krishan, an adherent to the Hindu faith and a resident of Coventry, not far from Leicester. With the exception of a brief period spent elsewhere, Ram has lived in Coventry since his arrival in the UK from the Punjab region of India in 1954. Below, I will briefly discuss some key points which are important to the understanding of his narrative.

Mr Krishan was nearly twenty-four years old when he arrived in Britain. However, in this narrative, he devotes a large part of his story to his life before reaching Britain. This is because his early years are of particular significance to him, and he must have kept these reliable 'memories' in his heart.

Thus, Mr Krishan recounts vivid stories about his elementary education in Calcutta (now Kolkata), where he was born, of his middle school education in Nawanshahr in the Punjab region, where he was evacuated during the Second World War, and of his education at the DAV (Dayanand Anglo Vernacular) College in Jalandhar. He also describes his family background. Mr Krishan lived in Calcutta and the Punjab region during particularly turbulent times, throughout the Second World War and the 1947 partitioning of India and Pakistan.[3] He lucidly recounts stories of political incidents and of politicians, while also recalling his reading of Indian literature (including poetry, which he adored). Readers who are interested in this era of history may wish to pursue further reading on the incidents, politicians and authors mentioned.

When Mr Krishan arrived in Britain, he went to Coventry and started to work at a factory belonging to Alfred Herbert Limited, one of the world's largest manufacturers and distributors of machine tools. Here, he experienced racial discrimination for the first time. Perhaps this was one reason why he began to attend meetings of the Indian

Workers' Association,[4] founded in Coventry in 1938. However, this was not a place where he felt altogether comfortable, so he and his friends founded the Indian Cultural and Welfare Society[5] in 1958/9, in order both to support immigrants from India and to encourage Indian cultural activities. He played an active part as one of the group's founding members. His story describes the lives and working environment of Indian immigrants in Coventry in the 1950s and discusses their cultural activities, a topic which has received little attention from scholars.

Mr Krishan is a follower of the Hindu faith who came from the Punjab region of India. The Punjab region is often associated more with Sikhism than Hinduism: indeed, it is often described as the 'homeland' of the Sikhs, and as a region with a majority Sikh population.[6] Readers may be familiar with the 1984 attack on the Golden Temple complex at Amritsar by the Indian Army and the subsequent assassination of the Indian Prime Minister, Mrs Indira Gandhi, by her two Sikh bodyguards.[7] Hindus are a substantial minority in the contemporary Indian state of Punjab, although relatively few scholars have written about them.[8] However, Sikhs were not, in fact, a majority in the Punjab until 1966, when it became a much smaller state after the creation of the separate state of Haryana (which consisted of a majority Hindi speaking population) and the assignment of some other areas to Himachal Pradesh. It is, however, inaccurate to consider the Punjab region as exclusively Sikh.[9] This is something I myself observed when I visited the Punjab for research.

In Leicester, which is the main focus of my field work research, most Hindus' families come from the Gujarat region. Hindus live in most other states of India too as the religious majority, and the UK's Hindu population now includes Hindus from many states of India as well as from Sri Lanka, Nepal and other places. A Hindu temple in Leicester called the Shree Geeta Bhavan Temple and Hindu Community Centre was opened in about 1985 by Punjabi Hindus, and remains in use today. It has its own unique history.[10] Punjabi Hindus have a unique history in Coventry, which Ram describes in his narrative.

The British government began to develop a multi-cultural policy from the second half of the 1970s onwards,[11] and these developments are relevant to Ram's own narrative, because he was involved in founding the Multi-Faith Forum in Coventry, and to its further development in later years. Similar initiatives have appeared in a number of cities, including Leicester.[12] The Coventry forum was established in the late 1990s, and is supported by the city council. Ram joined the Forum at its outset, and has participated each year in annual events such as the 'Peace Walk' (see Appendix 4, pp. 109–110). My understanding of this organisation was greatly enhanced when I visited it in August 2015, and interviewed its President, Mr Harry Hall, who was born in Jamaica. I have included the photos I took during that visit in this booklet.

The Multi-Faith Forum is one of a range of multicultural initiatives in Coventry, which include not only groups but also facilities such as multi-faith prayer rooms. Major hospi-

I   Introduction

tals have always traditionally had a Christian chapel on site, but after multicultural policies were implemented, multi-faith prayer rooms were established to accommodate not only Christians but also Jews, Hindus, Sikhs, Muslims and others. The multi-faith centre located on the ground floor of the Walsgrave University Hospital in Coventry possesses faith-specific prayer rooms for which advice was drawn from the Multi-Faith Forum.[13] Such facilities are now provided not only in hospitals but also in jails, police buildings, universities, airports and so on. Some readers may have made use of similar multi-faith prayer rooms at Heathrow Airport or know of the pioneering chaplaincy at the University of Derby.[14]

Mr Krishan's interest in peace and reconciliation work has a particularly poignant relationship to the history of Coventry, which suffered severe bombing during the Second World War, when the cathedral and much of the city were destroyed.[15]

Every year since 1989, a local Coventry group, the Lord Mayor's Peace Committee, has organized the Hiroshima Day Service and the Committee also organizes the Coventry Peace Festival.[16] Mr Krishan has been involved in these events annually as a member of the Multi-Faith Forum. In July 2006, the City of Coventry united with the City of Hiroshima, the first city in the world to experience the dropping of an atomic bomb, to form the 'Hiroshima Coventry Club'. This association was the initiative of Mrs Hideko Okamoto (see page 58). Professor Eleanor Nesbitt (Mr Krishan's wife) had brought Hideko and her husband Professor Toru Okamoto to the Hiroshima Day service soon after their arrival for a year at the University of Warwick in 2004. The Hiroshima Day Service is especially meaningful for Mr Krishan because of his memory of hearing the news on the day of the bombing of Hiroshima, which made him and countless other Indians at that time feel angry and powerless.

I have asked Eleanor to write a brief life story of her own, including a description of how she met her husband, and her narrative contributes greatly to our understanding of Mr Krishan's story. I am very grateful for her generous cooperation.

I first met Mr Ram Krishan in August 2011, when I visited Eleanor at their home.[17] As I was conversing with them both, I realised that he was a follower of the Hindu faith who came from the Punjab region, and so I became eager to hear his life story in greater detail. Next time I visited Eleanor I asked if I could interview him, and he willingly consented. I interviewed him four times, and then created a transcript based on the interview tapes, with the narrative categorized under thematic subheadings. I sent these for Ram to read and correct. I am very grateful not only to Ram but also to Eleanor for their cooperation during this process, because without their continuing support, this booklet would never have been published. During the editing process, I visited their home many times, and worked together with them over lunch. This was a very happy fulfilling time, which I remember fondly. I am truly grateful to them both for allowing me to share their time.

I Introduction

The foreword to this booklet is by Dr Pippa Virdee,[18] Senior Lecturer in Modern South Asian History in the School of Humanities at De Montfort University, Leicester. Dr Virdee's academic interests lie in the fields of British colonial history, the history of the Punjab, and the history of the South Asian Diaspora in Britain. She has also (like Professor Nesbitt before her) been the convener for the Punjab Research Group (PRG).[19] I invited Dr Virdee to write a foreword for this booklet because she lives in Coventry, and has a deep understanding of the history of the Punjab region and of immigrant communities in Coventry. She is also a good friend of Ram and Eleanor. I would like to extend my warmest gratitude to Dr Virdee for agreeing to write the foreword.

Notes

1 In 2010, I started to publish a series of booklets entitled the *Memory and Narrative Series*, as part of my work with the Research Centre for the History of Religious and Cultural Diversity, Meiji University, Tokyo, using material from interviews with members of various immigrant communities in Leicester. I have already published nine booklets. These include the life stories of a Caribbean woman, a Jewish woman, a Sikh woman, a Sikh artist and his wife, a Muslim businessman who came to Leicester via Uganda in 1972, a man of mixed heritage, a Latvian man and his wife, a Hindu man and an Indian Classical Dancer.

2 In 2011 I began to publish a series of articles entitled the *Discussion Paper Series*. I have already published seven such articles. They include discussions of oral history, and commentaries on the *Memory and Narrative Series, 1–8*.

3 For information on Indian Partition in 1947, see Vazira Fazila-Yacoobali Zamindar, *The Long Partition and the Making of Modern South Asia: Refugees, Boundaries, Histories*, New York: Columbia University Press, 2007; Yasmin Khan, *The Great Partition: The Making of India and Pakistan*, Yale, 2008; Ian Talbot and Gurharpal Singh, *The Partition of India*, Cambridge: Cambridge University Press, 2009; Panikos Panayi & Pippa Virdee (eds), *Refugees and the End of Empire: Imperial Collapse and Forced Migration during the Twentieth Century* (Basingstoke: Palgrave, 2011); Ian Talbot (ed.), *The Independence of India and Pakistan: New Approaches and Reflections*, Oxford: Oxford University Press, 2013. For India during the Second World War, see Yasmin Khan, *India at War: The Subcontinent and the Second World War*, Oxford: Oxford University Press, 2015.

4 The first Indian Workers' Association (IWA) was founded in London in the 1930s; another was established in Coventry in 1938. Immigrant workers from India came together to campaign for Indian independence. In 1958, the Indian Workers' Association (GB) was set up to provide a central national body coordinating the activities of local groups. It aimed to improve conditions for immigrant workers, working alongside the mainstream British labour movement. Most of its members were Sikhs. See John DeWitt, *Indian Workers' Associations in Britain*, Oxford: Oxford University Press, 1969; Sasha Josephides, *Towards a History of the Indian Workers' Association*, Coventry: Centre for Research in Ethnic Relations, University of

I   **Introduction**

Warwick, 1991; John King, *Three Asian Associations in Britain*, Coventry: University of Warwick, Centre for Research in Ethnic Relations, 1994; Pippa Virdee, *Coming to Coventry: Stories from the South Asian Pioneers*, Coventry Teaching PCT & The Herbert, 2006, pp. 59–65; Talvinder Gill, 'The Indian Workers' Association Coventry 1938–1990: Political and Social Action', *South Asian History and Culture*, Vol. 4, Issue 4, 2013.

5   For information about social activities within Asian groups, including the Indian Cultural and Welfare Society, see Pippa Virdee, *op. cit.*, pp. 93–105.

6   Gurharpal Singh, *Ethnic Conflict in India: A Case-Study of Punjab*, Basingstoke: Macmillan Press LTD, 2000, p. 88. See Table 5.1 Punjab's Area and Population, 1941–91.

7   For the 1984 attack on the Golden Temple and the subsequent assassination of the then Prime Minister Indira Gandhi by two Sikh bodyguards on the 31st October of the same year, see H. Kaur, *Blue Star over Amritsar: The Real Story of June 1984*, Corporate Vision: New Delhi, 2006; D. S. Tatla, *The Sikh Diaspora: The Search for Statehood*, London: UCL Press, 1999; Lt. Gen. K. S. Brar, *Operation Blue Star: The True Story*, UBSPD: New Delhi, 1993; P. R. Brass, *The Politics of India since Independence*, Cambridge: Cambridge: Cambridge University Press, 1990; R. Jeffrey, *What's Happening to India?: Punjab, Ethnic Conflict, Mrs Gandhi's Death and the Test for Federalism*, New York: Homes & Meier, 1986. See also Mark Tully and Satish Jacob, *Amritsar*, London: Jonathan Cape, 1985.

8   Eleanor Nesbitt, 'Hinduism in Punjab', in K. A. Jacobsen (ed.), *Brill's Encyclopedia of Hinduism*, volume 4, Leiden: Brill, 2012, pp. 573–587.

9   Gurharpal Singh, *op. cit.*, p. 88; See Table 5.1 Punjab's Area and Population, 1941–91.

10 This information was obtained during an interview with two Hindus [the late Mr. Mahesh Chandra Prasher (18th August 2003); the late Mr Paras Shridhar (21st August 2003) from the Punjab region of India at the Shree Geeta Bhavan, Leicester]; 'Punjabi Hindus plan city temple' (*Leicester Mercury*, 22 April 1985).

11 For a summary of the idea of multiculturalism, see Christina Julios, *Contemporary British Identity: English Language, Migrants and Public Discourse*, Aldershot: Ashgate, 2008.

12 The Leicester Council of Faiths was founded in 1986, for a similar reason to its sister group in Coventry. It celebrated its 20th anniversary in 2006. For the Leicester Council of Faiths, see *20th Anniversary Brochure for Leicester Council of Faiths, Souvenir Brochure 1986–2006*, Leicester: Leicester Council of Faiths, 2006. For information on the Multi-Faith Centre at the University of Derby, see http://www.communitydirectoryderbyshire.org.uk/view/21/the-multi-faith-centre-at-th... [accessed: 28 August 2016]. This information was also obtained during an interview with the Director of the Centre, Mrs Eileen Fry (9th August 2006 at the Centre).

13 Spiritual Care – University Hospitals Coventry (http://www.uhcw.nhs.ukforpatients-and-visitors/spritual-care).

14 For example, there are multi-faith rooms in each terminal at Heathrow, offering quiet places of retreat for prayer and meditation. For information on the Heathrow prayer rooms and chapel, see a leaflet called 'Heathrow Airport Chaplaincy: Caring

for the Whole Airport Community Passengers & Staff' (Chapel of St George & Multi-Faith Prayer Room); http://www.heathrow.com/airport-guide/terminal-facilities- and-services/prayer-rooms... [accessed: 28 August 2016]. For the Multi-faith Centre at the University of Derby, see note, no. 11.

15 For information on Coventry and the Second World War, see David McGrory, *Coventry at War*, The History Press, 1997; David McGrory, *Coventry's Blitz*, Stroud: Amberley, 2015; http://www.historiccoventry.co.uk/cathedrals/ruins-now.php [accessed: 23 June 2015].

16 For information on the Hiroshima Coventry Club, see 'Hiroshima Friendship Link with Coventry: Hiroshima Coventry Club' (http://www7b.biglobe.ne.jp/~coventryclub/eghirocov.html) [accessed: 28 August 2016]. For the photos of Hiroshima Day 2016, see http://coventrycityofpeace.uk/hiroshima-day-photo-2016 [accessed: 5 October 2016]

17 Eleanor Nesbitt's publications include: (with K. Puri) *Pool of Life: The Autobiography of a Punjabi Agony Aunt*, Brighton: Sussex Academic Press, 2013; 'Sikh Diversity in the UK: Contexts and Evolution' in K. A. Jacobsen and K. Myrvold (eds), *Sikhs in Europe: Migration, Identities and Representations*, Aldershot: Ashgate, pp. 225–252; With Doris R. Jakobsh 'Sikhism and Women: Contexualizing the Issues', in Doris R. Jakobsh (ed.), *Sikhism and Women: History, Texts and Experience*, Oxford: Oxford University Press, 2010, pp. 1–39; *Sikhism: a Very Short Introduction*, Oxford: Oxford University Press, 2005; *Intercultural Education: Ethnographic and Religious Approaches*, Brighton: Academic Press, 2004; *The Religious Lives of Sikh Children: A Coventry Based Study*, Leeds: Community Religious Project, University of Leeds, 2000; 'Section C: Sikhism', in P. Morgan and C. A. Lawton (eds), *Ethical Issues in Six Religious Traditions*, Edinburgh: Edinburgh University Press, 1996, pp. 118–167; 'The Transmission of Christian Tradition in an Ethnically Diverse Society', in Rohit Barot (ed.), *op.cit.*, pp. 156–169; 'Valmikis in Coventry: the Revival and Reconstruction of a Community', in R. Ballard (ed.), *op.cit.*, pp. 117–141; 'The Presentation of Sikhs in Recent Children's Literature in Britain', in I. T. O'Connell, M. Israel and W. G. Oxtoby (eds), *Sikh History and Religion in the Twentieth Century*, Toronto: University of Toronto, 1988, pp. 376–387; With D. S. Tatla (eds), *Sikhs in Britain: an Annotated Bibliography*, Coventry: Centre for Research in Ethnic Relations, University of Warwick, 1987. For more of Eleanor Nesbitt's articles and books see http://www2.warwick.uk/fac/soc/ces/research/wreru/aboutus/staff/en/ [28 August 2016]. Eleanor is also author of 'Oral History and the Study of Religions: Reflections on Professor Kiyotaka Sato's Memory and Narrative Series', *Discussion Paper* [Research Centre for the History of Religious and Cultural Diversity, Meiji University, Tokyo], no. 6, 2015, pp. 1–26.

18 Dr Virdee's main publications include: 'Dreams, Memories and Legacies: Partitioning India' in Knut Jacobsen (ed.), *Routledge Handbook of Contempary India*, (Routledge, 2015); 'No-mans Land' and the Creation of Partitioned Histories in India/Pakistan in Nigal Eltringham and Pam Maclean (eds), *Remembering Genocide*, Series Title: Remembering The Modern World, General Editors: David Lowe and Tony Joel (Routledge, 2014); 'Remembering Partition: Women, Oral Histories and

I **Introduction**

    the Partition of 1947', *Oral History*, vol. 41, no. 2, 2013, pp. 49–62; With Panikos Panayi (eds), *Refugees and the End of Empire: Imperial Collapse and Forced Migration during the Twentieth Century* (Basingstoke: Palgrave, 2011); 'Negotiating the Past: Journey through Muslim Women's Experience of Partition and Resettlement', *Cultural and Social History*, vol. 6, no. 4, 2009, pp. 467–484; 'Partition in Transition: Comparative Analysis of Migration in Ludhiana and Lyallpur', in A. Gera and N. Bhatia (eds), *Partitioned Lives: Narratives of Home, Displacement and Resettlement* (Delhi: Pearson, 2007), pp. 156–173; 'Partition and the Absence of Communal Violence in Malerkotla', in I. Talbot (ed.), *The Deadly Embrace: Religion and Violence in the Indian Subcontinent 1947–2002* (Karachi: UP, 2007); *Coming to Coventry: Stories from the South Asian Pioneers* (Coventry: The Herbert, 2006); for her articles and books in detail, see http://www.dmu.ac.uk/about=dmu/academic-staff/art-design-humanities/pippa-virdee.aspx [2 December 2016].

19 The Punjab Research Group (PRG) is a body of independent, interdisciplinary scholars engaged in Punjab Studies. It was established early in 1984. One of the aims of the PRG when it was established was to create dialogue between the 'three Punjabs': East Punjab, West Punjab and the Punjab Diaspora (www.theprg.co.uk). The same year saw the attack on the Golden Temple complex (especially Akal Takhat) at Amritsar by the Indian Army in June 1984; the assassination of the Indian prime minister Indira Gandhi by her two Sikh bodyguards on 31st October and the subsequent anti-Sikh riots; and the emergence of the Khalistan movement which campaigned for an independent Punjab. Professor Eleanor Nesbitt is one of the founders of the PRG.

II
The Life Story of Mr Ram Krishan (Prashar)

II The Life Story of Mr Ram Krishan (Prashar)

1 Life in Kolkata (Calcutta)[1] and my primary education

Mr Ram Krishan[2] was born in Calcutta in British India in 1931 and lived there until he was ten or eleven years old. He recalls that time thus:

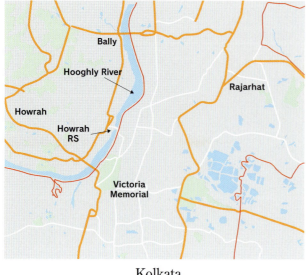

Kolkata

I was born in Calcutta, India on the 5th October 1931. My father was working in Calcutta in a Marwari[3] firm. He was a manager. In Calcutta I was living in Salkia, where I went to school. It is near the Howrah railway station, the station near River Hooghly – when you cross the Hooghly River, on the other side is Calcutta. (At that time Calcutta had no railway station named 'Calcutta'.)

We knew that our grandfather and grandmother were in Nawanshahr (in Punjab). When we went to Nawanshahr we always used to go by train. Father arranged the travel in such a way that, before reaching Nawanshahr, we would visit Ayodhya, Banaras, Mathura, Vrindavan and other religious places which came along the way. It normally took two or three weeks.

I saw my grandfather and grandmother when my *mundan sanskar* [ritual head-shaving] happened. I was probably three years old. I remember that we went to Jwalamukhi[4] by bullock cart. I remember all my head was shaved. It felt very odd to me. Until then I had had long hair. After shaving my head, I had a bath in *suraj kund* [a tank of water] in the temple and I put on new clothes. Sweetmeats were distributed and we were staying in our priest's house in Jwalaji [another name for Jwalamukhi]. Jwalaji was a beautiful town in the hills. There was a story that Mughal emperor Akbar [1542–1605] paid homage to Jwalaji.

We used to come back to Calcutta after two or three months. It was a good routine: Father [would] come to Nawanshahr and he could take as much time as he wanted.

In Salkia the atmosphere in our house was very religious. I still remember that we brothers [my younger brother, Hari Krishan and I] used to get up early in the morning and we were taught to touch the feet of our father and mother (a sign of respect in Hindu tradition). Before that we used to open our hands and, looking at our palms, we used to recite a mantra:

II   The Life Story of Mr Ram Krishan (Prashar)

karagre vaste lakshmi
karmadhayay saraswati
karmule tu govindam
prabhate karadarshanam

This means: At the tip of my hand dwells Goddess Lakshmi [goddess of wealth, fortune and prosperity, both material and spiritual]; in the middle of my hand dwells Goddess Saraswati [goddess of knowledge and arts, embodying the wisdom of Devi]. At the base of my hand dwells Sri Govinda [one of the names of Vishnu]. Early in the morning I contemplate (the deities in) my hands.

Then, before putting our feet on the floor, we used to recite:

samudra vasne devi
parvatastane mandale
vishnu patni namastubhyam
padasparsham kshamasvame.

'Bauji', my father, Pandit Malawa Ram. This photo was probably taken before I was born.

This means: Goddess [i.e. Earth] who is clothed in the sea and who is adorned with the mountains, who is the wife of Vishnu [one of the most significant deities in Hinduism], I greet you. Forgive me for setting foot on you. Then my brother and I used to touch our father's and mother's feet.

Then my father and both of us brothers used to go to the bank of the Hooghly, which was a stone's throw from our house, and bath in the river Hooghly. (The river Ganges is called Hooghly in Calcutta and is regarded as sacred.)

Usually Father used to worship the rising sun with flowers and water from [the] Hooghly and we used to return to our house with a bucket full of water. There our mother had a *thali* [metal plate] ready of *puja samagri* – flowers, rice, *mauli* [red thread]. There was a small square table [*chaunki*]. On top of that were *murti*s [images of gods] [and] a *jot* [little oil light]. Mother had spread three *kusha* [grass] mats on which me, my brother, mother and sister used to sit and a fourth was for my father in the middle, and we all used to worship deities of Lord Shiva, Durga (Goddess of Strength) and Ganesh (God of wisdom).

After the *puja* Father, [my] brother and I always used to recite some chapters [from the] Bhagavad Gita.[5] After reciting the Gita, Father read to us from other religious books like *Vishnu Puran* [*Vishnu Purana*, an important religious text] and we used to listen with respect. After the worship *prasad* (blessed food) was given to us and we [would]

II The Life Story of Mr Ram Krishan (Prashar)

have our breakfast which was always prepared by my mother.

Then we went to school and Father used to go to attend his work. Sometimes, before going to school, we brothers used to attend the Satyanarayan Temple and have *darshan* [a glimpse and blessing] of the deity.

In the evening we [would] go to Satyanarayan Temple, which was only five minutes walk from our house, and used to attend the *arati* [ritual involving circling of a light in front of the deities] there. In the evening our father would help us with our homework from school and then we used to go to sleep. This was our daily routine and in that process I really learned that chapter of Gita which is 'Vishwarupa Darshan' [chapter 11 in which Krishna manifests his universal form], the favourite of my father.

I heard a very interesting story about the Satyanarayan Temple. My father told me that Bara Babu (his boss) told him (because he was a devotee of Hinduism) he had a dream one night that Satyanarayan Bhagvan [God Vishnu as embodiment of truth] appeared and he said to him, 'I want you to erect a temple for me and there is a particular [plot of] land where I want it to be built.' So when he woke up he enquired about the land and he found out that it belonged to a Muslim chap. That area was called Salkia Banda Ghat. Anyway, he called that man and requested land for erecting a Hindu temple and he refused. So Bara Babu was sad and it was postponed. [The] story goes that, after six months or a year, that chap came again and met Bara Baba and he said, 'A very strange thing happened, I had a dream last night and some holy man [was] saying to me, "You should allow Bara Babu to erect that Hindu temple there, but also request him that he should build a mosque thereabout."' Bara Babu was very happy. So that is how the Satyanarayan Temple was built and, just near the corner – five or ten minutes walk from that temple – he paid all the expenses for erecting the mosque. It shows how amicable relations between Hindus and Muslims were in that locality. I don't know how far it is true, but that is the story my father told me.

Sometimes we used to go to Lilwa on our morning walk. That was a small village and the garden of Thakur Das Sureka, the boss where my father used to work. Father also used to take us to Victoria Memorial [a large marble building built between 1906 and 1921 dedicated to the memory of Queen Victoria (1819–1901)] and other places of interest in Calcutta. Those were very good and happy days.

The house where we were living was [a] two- or three-storey building, and we never used to pay any rent for that because it was owned by Thakur Das Sureka. There were other tenants also in the house and Father used to collect rent from them and keep account of that and give it to his boss. In exchange for that we were allowed to live free.

Sometimes I used to go where my father used to work. We used to call his office '*gaddi*', meaning that it was a floor covered with nice white sheets, and three or four *munni*s (account keepers) used to work there. Next door Father used to work, with table, chairs and telephone. It was quite a big building and on the third floor there was a kitchen where vegetarian food [was] cooked and sometimes we two would eat there.

My primary education

The name of my primary school was Satyanarayan Madhav Mishra Vidyalaya, where I studied up to fourth or fifth class. I started to learn Sanskrit and Hindi in primary school and we used to speak Punjabi in the house: I had three or four languages – English, Hindi, Sanskrit and [later] Urdu. I used to read poems and novels – whatever was in a book I used to read: it might be a detective novel or a story or a poem. That is how I studied. I remember in the school there was a picture of Maharana Pratap[Singh],[6] Shivaji [Bhonsle][7] and Guru Gobind Singh.[8] Sometimes Father used to address the students. One teacher was a Rajput (warrior caste): he wore a turban. On one special occasion he tied a turban on me.

I was quite good in my studies and I remember winning many prizes [at the] annual gathering. I was a brainy student, especially in the classical language Sanskrit – like Latin. [Father] was very happy with our school reports. Sometimes when I [went] to the temple I [would] meet a holy man who used to sit on the deerskin, and that holy man [was] very happy with me, [saying], 'At this tender age you know so much about Hindu religion.'

I didn't have many friends and most of the time I used to read and there were a lot of Hindi books in our house and magazines which Father used to bring. I remember Hindi magazines called *Sudha*, *Madhuri* and *Chand*. These were very prominent literary magazines along with *Hindu Panch* and *Matwala*. My father used to go to Shree Hanuman Pustakalaya (library). I used to go in the evening sometimes with my father and at a very early age I used to read the Hindi newspaper *Vishwamitra*.

In our house we had three rooms downstairs and in the last room (Father's office) was Father's chair, table and *almari*s [steel cupboards] full of these books and magazines, a good library of two to three hundred books, and Father encourage[d] us in reading and writing. In my spare time I used to go to the office and read. His friends [would] come and sit in the office and drink tea prepared by my mother.

I used to read [the] Hindi newspaper every day and so I knew what [was] happening in the country, that India [was] fighting for independence. I had interest in political happenings in India – even from that age. I remember that one day I read the front-page headline: 'Viceroy[9] sent Gandhi[10] away empty-handed.' I came home and told my mother, 'Mama, Viceroy did a mean thing to Gandhiji. He let Gandhi go empty-handed. He never gave him any *shagun*.' (There is a tradition in India that when someone meets a respected person for the first time he always gives money.) Mother laughed a lot.

My father was respected a lot in Salkia's community. There used to be a literary club

II The Life Story of Mr Ram Krishan (Prashar)

and he was a very active member there. Sometimes he used to take me to those meetings. I could not understand much but I knew poetry was being read and there used to be a nice discussion. There was one learned man whom we used to call Shastriji. I think he was from Kashi Vidyapith which was a kind of learned association in Banaras. He always used to praise me, 'Look [at] this boy, he's always reading.'

I remember Swami Karpatriji's visit [in 1941] to our school (he was a prominent saint at that time) and other holy men used to visit our school. I also vividly remember that once, from that road going to our house, when we were coming in the evening from our walk, on the other side of the Hooghly river I saw flames. I asked my father, 'What is that?' Father told me, 'This is from the funeral pyre of Rabindranath Tagore.'[11]

We used to celebrate Diwali, Janmashtami [12] and, in the month of Sravan, [13] the temple [would] be illuminated. There was a little garden near the temple and I remember, on the Sharad Purnima, in a big pot they used to prepare the rice pudding the whole night while the full moon was shining. In the morning that *prasad* (a food for a religious offering) [was] served to the devotees and there used to be quite a crowd dancing and singing near the temple.

My father was very sympathetic to the Congress movement and he told me that he attended the Haripura sessions of [the] All India National Congress in March 1938 [14] where Subhash Chandra Bhose [15] was president that year, and there he saw various leaders of Congress: Jawaharlal Nehru, [16] Rajendra Prasad, [17] Sardar Patel, [18] Maulana Azad [19] etc. He flew there in a small aeroplane.

He told me a very interesting story about Gandhiji. Gandhi was visiting Bengal. At that time Gandhi was campaigning about teaching Hindi to non-Hindi-speaking people. So he gave an advert in a paper for people to teach Bengalis Hindi language. Father read that advert and applied for a volunteer job. He received a reply from Gandhi's secretary telling him the date and the time of the appointment to meet Gandhiji. At the appointed time Gandhiji called my father and said, 'Do you speak Bengali?' Father said, 'No.' He said. 'How will you teach Hindi to Bengalis then?' Father replied, 'I know English very well and I will teach Hindi by using English'. For a second Gandhi was silent and then he said to my father, 'Well, that is teaching English, not Hindi.' Then Father explained that slowly, slowly as they learn Hindi the English will cease. Gandhi replied very tersely to my father, 'How long have you been living in Bengal?' He said, 'Ten years.' 'You are living in Bengal for ten years and you do not know Bengali?' My father was silent. Gandhi called his secretary. He said, 'Write his name as a volunteer.' And then [Father said], 'He said to me, "Go and learn Bengali" and dismissed me.' It showed how careful Gandhi was about the importance of mother tongue and the national language.

[In the] mean time a *seth* [wealthy businessman] came to see him (Gandhiji) and wanted a message of good wishes for his business. Gandhi said, 'What is your trade as a businessman?' he said, 'I sell *tamaku* [tobacco].' So Gandhi took a paper out and wrote down

II The Life Story of Mr Ram Krishan (Prashar)

'Smoking is dangerous for health.' He signed and gave the paper to that rich man. The man was very embarrassed and bowed to Gandhiji and left the room very quickly. Father picked up the paper and brought it home and for years we treasured it. Father was full of praise for Gandhiji. That was how my political awakening was progressing.

When the mango season came Father used to buy a lot of mangos. We used to put them in a bucket full of cold water. [We] all used to sit around the bucket and suck the mangos and after that used to drink buttermilk. On a weekly basis Father used to call [the] seller of *dalmot* [spicy mix of fried lentils and chickpea vermicelli], *dahi bara* [pulse flour dumplings in yoghurt] and sweets to the house and everyone would enjoy [them].

Father was a very hardworking man. I remember that, after coming from work, he used to go to one rich man's office who was a wholesale soap dealer and he used to earn a little bit of money for that, along with free soap delivery to the house. The pieces of soap [were] big and round for washing the clothes.

He [Father] never used to give us money but always used to say, 'What do you want?' Anything we wanted he used to supply it. He always used to say, 'Cut your coat according to your cloth.'

We used to visit Kali Ghat (a famous temple) and were thrilled to take part in Durga Puja[20] activities. There used to be a big procession of statues of Durga in the Durga Puja festivals. From the school we used to celebrate Ganesh Puja and all of us in a row used to take the statue of Ganesh, singing hymns, and take that to the Hooghly river and immerse [it].

I remember my father was very kind to all the tenants and, many times, the family of those who were living there. Father [would] take them on a boat ride and we [would] go to Rani Ras Manika Baghicha where Ramakrishna Paramahansa[21] used to meditate, or any nice place where Father entertain[ed] all of us with sweets and, if the weather was warm, a picnic. So the relationship with [the tenants] was very, very cordial. They used to respect and love my father very much.

I still remember, when we left Calcutta and were living in Nawanshahr, one of the tenants, who was from UP [i.e. what is now Uttar Pradesh state], used to send gifts to us, although so many years had passed. I remember one of the ladies who was very fond of me. She took me to her father's house and asked my mum if she could take care of me as she did not have any child of her own. They used to assist my mum in cooking and other things. One day a neighbouring house caught fire and my father, although he was thin [meaning weak], went inside to save a boy and dragged him outside from the burning house while many people were standing watching. People [were] telling me, 'Panditji has gone in, Panditji has gone in,' and he was very much praised in the locality.

On 4th September 1939 [the second] World War started and the price of food went up in

II The Life Story of Mr Ram Krishan (Prashar)

the market. We were told that Japan may bombard Calcutta. All kinds of rumours were in the air. We all were thinking, 'What is going to happen?' [and] whether we [would be] staying in Calcutta or not. Many people were leaving Calcutta and we were witnessing blackout at night. Father was talking about moving to Nawanshahr.

I remember in the Second World War the blackout at night because there was fear of Japanese air attacks. We saw that food prices were going up and the necessities of life were disappearing from the market. A lot of people were leaving Calcutta and going to other parts of India. I heard that the government of India said that the city of Calcutta should be evacuated so that the civilian casualties would be less. We decided to leave Calcutta and go to Punjab in the northern part of India.

2 Life in Nawanshahr: my family and my secondary education

Mr Krishan moved to Nawanshahr in Punjab from Calcutta in 1941. He talks of his family background and remembers his education there. This is how he recalls it:

My family in Nawanshahr

We moved from Calcutta to Nawanshahr in [the] Punjab region in 1941 because World War II (1939 to 1945) took place. We were a bit scared that at any time there could be a siren and that the Japanese were coming in force. We left at the end of 1941.

When I came to Nawanshahr I heard from the people (and I think I read also somewhere) about Nawanshahr:

nawanshahr ki char chizen hai khari
gur, shivala, rerian, bara dari.

[In other words] Nawanshahr is famous for: raw sugar, a big temple of Lord Shiva (Banamal ka Shivala), sesame-studded sweets, (and) a big walled park, which was there even in the time of [the 6th Mughal] Emperor Aurangzeb [Alamgir (1618–1707, his reign: 1658–1707)], with towers (*burji*) and twelve gates.

About eight or ten miles [away] was a village called Rahon and when Banda Bahadar [22] [who led the Sikhs after Guru Gobind Singh] was fighting, he came as far as Rahon – or so I heard.

We settled in the Punjab in Nawanshahr because my grandfather and his family were living there. He had a house, so we were all living there.

I have already said what sort of person my father was. His thinking was liberal. He told us we should be good citizens and good men, respect all religions and respect the elders

II The Life Story of Mr Ram Krishan (Prashar)

and the standards that at that time society was observing. He said, 'You should think things out fairly.'

My mother was a noble, patient and very kind lady. She used to cook nice food for us [and] always take care of us. She was a good companion to my father. When my father went back to Calcutta and she was in Nawanshahr, all that time she was running the house efficiently. My father used to send the money and my mother kept an eye that all things should be in order – food, clothes, going to school and how we [were] learning. My mother was like a home minister. [She] had a very strong personality; she was courageous, kind and very fond of reading Hindi books and religious literature, [and] she was a devotee, as [a] Hindu religious house demands.

Mataji, my mother, Rattan Devi, as I remember her in Nawanshahr, Punjab.

I remember my father telling me that when he was working in Calcutta in a small firm, before he joined Thakurdas Sureka Limited, Salkia, a mischief-maker alleged some mismanagement of the funds. My father was very upset because, being a religious and God-fearing man, he [would] never do that, even in a dream. Naturally, he told my mother this incident. She was very furious and requested to meet his boss. In those days it was unthinkable that a woman [could] do a thing like that. So, when my father went to work, my mother followed him and eventually met his boss and said, 'Look, we will never do this kind of mean things which your employee is saying about my husband. But even if it is proved we will pay it back.' It was a very impressive occurrence. Father's boss was impressed by her straightforwardness and he called that mischief-maker and [asked whether he was] saying the right thing. After a lot of argument that chap admitted that he had done this because he was jealous of my father's position. The boss sacked him and praised my mother. It was a very rare thing at that time that a lady from a distant province will do that. After that, Father said, 'You said you will pay back, but we are not in a position to pay it back. How would we do that?' She said, 'We would have sold the jewellery.'

Here I also remember that there was a time in the family when we were in Nawanshahr when we were going through a terrible financial period. She did give her gold bangles and some jewellery and Father went to Amritsar, where her sister used to live, and they sold the jewellery, and with that money we arranged our housekeeping. But after that, when my father saved a bit of money, he bought them back.

II The Life Story of Mr Ram Krishan (Prashar)

She [my mother] was from Kartarpur and it was a famous place because of the Sodhi family, and the Kartarpurwali *bir* [original copy of the Sikh scriptures, compiled by the fifth Guru, Guru Arjan],[23] used to be kept in the fort. I heard that my *nana* [maternal grandfather] was *purohit* (family priest) of Kartarpur's guru and my mother told me that once, when the Akalis[24] [the Akali Movement] besieged Kartarpur, they demanded that the ownership of the Kartarpurwali *bir* should be given to them. Maharani Sahiba was very worried. She called my *nana* and said that there might be some trouble. She was very much worried about the safety of the Kartarpurwali *bir* and asked my *nana* what to do. My *nana* replied, 'If you think it is proper for me to take the Kartarpurwali *bir* to my place I will take this holy book – which is my holy book [too] – and place it in my house and nobody can move that from my house. It could be done only on my dead body.' Maharani was very much impressed and she agreed that he should do that. It was the time when Punjab was gripped by the Akali Movement.

My *nanaji* did this – he took it to his house in an appropriate way and put it in a corner of the house where holy things used to be put, and after some time there was some negotiation between Maharani and the Akalis and the Kartarpurwali *bir* went to the rightful place.

When I was small I visited the place with my father and I also had *darshan* of the Kartarpurwali *bir*. My mother said that my mother's brother, whose name was Ram Rakha, he told this story to my mum and my mum told me.

Mother said to me that any marriage which happened in my *khandan* [family], after the marriage the bride and bridegroom used to *matha tek* [pay obeisance] in the gurdwara. This was the custom.

Mother used to tell me many stories from Sikh mythology. So, from childhood, I knew quite a lot about Sikh history and particularly about the Kartarpurwali *bir*. My mother used to read Sukhmani Sahib (or perhaps it was Japji Sahib)[25] in the morning and used to tell me the stories of Sikh Gurus. Mother's sister, whom I called Masi, live[d] in Amritsar and, in the holidays, I used to visit her. They had a shop in Namakmandi: it sold *muraba* [sweet fruit preserve] and perfumes. In the morning we both used to visit Harmandir Sahib or Darbar Sahib (Golden Temple) and spend some time there. Then we used to go to Durgiana Mandir [temple to the Goddess][26] and come back to our house, and she used to feed me with *amle ka muraba* [preserve made from Indian gooseberries]. She love[d] me very much because she didn't have her own son. I had a lovely time there and still have a vivid memory of visiting Harmandir Sahib and Durgiana Mandir.

I also visited Jallianwala Bagh[27] when I used to be in Amritsar and came to know about General Dyer's butchery[28] of unarmed Indians in 1919. Mother used to tell me stories of Jallianwala Bagh, Lala Lajpat Rai[29] and Dr [Saifuddin] Kitchlew[30] who used to be a great Congress leader. I remember a Punjabi song which was prominent in 1919:

II The Life Story of Mr Ram Krishan (Prashar)

Kitchlew bira mere dukhre na phol
ramnavami si ayi Dyer goli chalai
mare kai anbhol.

O Brother Kitchlew, you don't listen to my woeful stories. The day of Ramnawami (a Hindu festival, celebrating the birth of God Rama) came and Dyer shot all the innocent people [in Jallianwala Bagh].

My father told me that no child used to live [i.e. survive] in our *khandan* because my grandfather [his father] was a tantric [a follower of Tantrism or tantric religion, an ancient Indian tradition of ritual practices]. He was also very respected. He was a *purohit* in Nawanshahr. He was a devotee of Goddess Durga and was very popular among Jats (farmer caste), and he used to do their marriage ceremony and other rituals. He was a very simple man, but there used to be a curse with his tantric thing: his guru said that [he could not] start living a normal *grihasthi*'s [i.e. family man's] life unless and until he [left] the tantric rituals, and my grandmother was very upset about his behaviour and tantric acts. So one day he agreed and vowed, 'From this day, I will not do any tantric acts and will [only] do Hindus' normal *puja path* [i.e. conduct customary acts of worship].'

However, when my father was born, my grandmother did not believe him. She wrapped my father in cloths, left the house and went to a nearby mosque. There was a *pir* there and she [put the] newly born child in his lap. [The] *pir* was bewildered and said, 'What is this? What is this?' She bowed her head and said, 'You keep him safe.'

When he removed the clothes he found a newborn baby and he said, 'Well, it is given by Maula (*parmatma*) [i.e. God]. So I give [him] back to you. May he live long!' My grandmother came home with the baby. [The] baby never died. When he was four or five years old my grandmother took him to the nearby Arya school, and the man who was admitting the children, his name was Bhadra Sain, he said, 'What is his name?' So Grandmother said, 'We call him 'Maula.' Being an Arya Samaji,[31] Bhadra Sainji said, 'What is this name "Maula?" I will write his name as "Malawa Ram."' (My grandfather's name was Atma Ram. So it went well.) So, he was admitted to the school and after that two more sons were born. Their names were Bhagauti Prashad and Padam Prakash. Many years later, as he had no son, [Padam Prakash] went to a gurdwara in Delhi and he promised to become a Sikh if, by Waheguru's [a Sikh name for God] grace, a son was born. A son was born and he became a Sikh.

My grandfather was determined to give a good education to his sons. At that time, after primary school, education up till matriculation was fee-paying. So my grandfather sold a bit of land for the purpose of giving education to his sons. At that time it was a very courageous and farsighted act. He never wanted his sons [to] do the *purohitai* [work as a priest]. And it happened that they never did the *purohitai* but, as I [have] told, the atmosphere of the house in Calcutta, and throughout life, was very strict *sanatan dharmi* [traditional Hindu].

II   The Life Story of Mr Ram Krishan (Prashar)

My sister, Satyabhama and her husband, Desh Mittar, soon after their marriage in Nawanshahr, Punjab, 1958.

Everybody called my grandfather '*bhakta*' (devotee). He used to get up 3 o'clock in the morning and it was [a] usual saying in the street – in our *mohalla* – that if anyone used to ask the time the other would reply, 'It must be 3 o'clock because Bhakta has just gone out to worship in the temple.'

He also had a medicine which he said [he had] obtained from a tantric guru to cure the smallpox. When he was called [to] the households of the sufferers he used to give that medicine to the parents of the children. If [the household was] Muslim he used to say, 'When he or she is cured, have some *rerian* [sesame-studded sweets] and dried fruit and a bit of money and give [these] to a Hindu girl' – *kanjakan* – that means small Hindu girls between [the] age of three to nine or ten. If the household was Hindu, he used to say, 'When the children are cured, call the Brahmin girls, give them clothes, cooked food and a bit of money.' So he was quite famous in Nawanshahr.

My grandmother was a very nice old lady. She used to tell me stories and then when I came to England she died. I was very sad, I couldn't do anything. In those days you couldn't easily go [back] to India. I still remember her, she was a very kind and loving lady.

I [have] got one brother and one sister. I am the oldest in the family. Like me, my brother studied at Arya High School, Nawanshahr and later on at DAV (Dayanand Anglo Vernacular) College, Jalandhar. He studied Sanskrit and all the other subjects, physics and mathematics, English, geography and history. He finished his university exam, and then he studied chartered accountancy. He became a chartered accountant and [later] became a bank manager. One of his sons lives in America where he is a vet. One son has a pharmacy and the other is a school teacher. Now my brother is retired, leading a peaceful life in Nawanshahr.

My sister studied in Nawanshahr Primary School. After that she studied [in] Kanya Mahavidyalaya in Nawanshahr. Then she went [on] to [pass] an exam in Hindi. She was bright, she came first in [the] Hindi exam (*prabhakar*) [the highest examination before studying for BA] in Punjab, Himachal Pradesh and Patiala. Her marriage was arranged to a very educated man and they lived in Ludhiana. Then they came to England and settled in Loughborough. She is now living near Cambridge with her daughter and son-in-law.

II The Life Story of Mr Ram Krishan (Prashar)

My secondary education

I was admitted in Arya High School in [the] sixth class. The school hours were 9 am–4 pm in the winter and 6 am–12 [noon] in the summer. We went to school [on] foot. School started with a prayer, then we went to classes: mathematics, English – an ordinary school timetable. I used to learn mathematics – trigonometry and geometry. Every day there was a drill. We also played football, hockey, cricket and an Indian game [mainly in Punjab region] called *kabaddi*.

History/geography was taught in Urdu [a Hindi speaker can understand spoken Urdu. It is the script that is different.] and I never knew [how to write] Urdu, so I was given special permission: whenever [the] teacher [taught] a lesson in Urdu I used to write whatever he was saying in Hindi. Then I started learning Urdu, after some time, at home and my father used to teach me Urdu script, so sooner or later I started to read Urdu.

I was so very good in Sanskrit and Hindi I was a class monitor until 10th class. It was a very good school and the standards were very high. I sometimes used to take the class if it was Sanskrit or Hindi. When Teacher used to come, I said, 'Stand up!' and all the boys would stand up and Teacher would start teaching.

I also got school prizes many times because I was good at Sanskrit and Hindi. There was also religious education and I used to come first in that. Once in [a] school exam in Sanskrit *dharma shiksha* (religious education) [the] teacher gave me 95 over 100. All the questions I answered correctly, so I asked him, 'Why [have] you deducted five marks?' So he said, 'Because your handwriting was bad.' He said, 'I can't give you 100 over 100.'

I was not good at mathematics, [so when there] was a school exam I was very worried and I was praying to Mataji (Mother Goddess): 'What's going to happen?' and it was the middle of the night in Nawanshahr at my house and Father was at that time in Calcutta, working, and we – all the family – [were] in Nawanshahr. So, it was very strange that I heard somebody saying that 'You go to the *bere* (courtyard, part of the house without a roof) and raise your head, seeing the moon, and come back and open your mathematics book.' So I did [this]. I went outside, saw the moon, came inside, opened the book and, on the right hand side of the page, there were six or seven questions. I was surprised in the morning, when I went to school and the question paper was delivered, all those six questions were there. I did that and that's how I passed my mathematics exam – very strange. After many years I told this story to my father. He was a bit angry and said, 'Never believe these kind of things. It is better that you study hard.' But it happened.

II The Life Story of Mr Ram Krishan (Prashar)

3 World War II (1939–1945) and the Partition of India in 1947

Mr Krishan experienced World War II and the Partition of India in 1947. This is how he remembers them.

World War II

Food and clothing were rationed. We had ration cards in the Punjab. In the shops around 1941 there was a black market. If you had a bit more money you could buy extra things. Our exercise books and slate pencils were also rationed. If you wanted more sugar you gave people more money and they would give you sugar. It was the first time I heard the word 'black market'. The rich people could buy things whereas the common people could not buy things.

We used to listen to the German radio (although it was banned) in Punjabi – German war propaganda, saying that we should agitate against the English, So we knew what was happening. Many Indians thought that the Germans would win and that we would get independence, but it was all wrong. It was propaganda from the German side. Indians were fighting for independence and were not sympathetic with the British government. It is true that there were many Indians who were joining the British Army, but this was for economic reasons. A million Indians were involved in the world war. [32]

We were in Punjab which is in the northern part of India. All the fighting was in the remote eastern part – Calcutta and even further, Burma – all those areas. From Burma the Japanese Army was fighting. There was also a national leader called Subhash Chandra Bose (see note 14, page 62) and Japan was supporting him. He formed the Indian National Army, fighting in Burma, up to Kohima [and] Imphal.

I do remember, I think it was in 1945 on the 6th August, when the atom bomb was dropped on Hiroshima and Nagasaki and people were stunned. We didn't like it. I do remember that. I was at school and we heard about the atomic bomb dropping on Hiroshima and we said it was very, very bad. Generally there was a great sympathy for Japan because of Subhash Chandra Bose.

The war ended [in] 1945. VE Day (Victory in Europe Day, 8 May 1945) was declared. The King made his speech on [the] radio. Churchill roared. When the end of [the] war was declared, the general people were not so happy. In India we did not know what was going to happen about India's independence. There was a victory parade and a victory celebration: the authorities distributed sweets and the students threw the sweets back at them, showing that we were not happy with British rule. There was a strong element of patriotism.

When India became independent there was a lot of rejoicing. We all were very happy [and] distributed sweets. But it was also the most shameful and blackest part of India's history. Thousands of people were uprooted from their homes, killed... women were raped. Houses were burned. Trains were attacked. It was genocide on both sides.

At that time, a famous woman poet of Punjabi, Amrita Pritam,[33] wrote the poem which represented the sentiments of all sane Indians:

aj akhan waris shah nun tu kabron vichon bol
te aj kitabe ishak da koi agla varka khol
roi si thi panjab di tu likh likh mare vain
aj lakhan thian rondian waris shah tainun kahin

I am asking Waris Shah [the Shakespeare of Punjabi Literature][34] who is in the grave, 'Speak up and turn over the page of the love story you wrote [i.e. *Hir Ranjha*]. One daughter of Punjab wept [a reference to Hir's plight]. You have written page after page describing her plight. Now hundreds of thousands of daughters are weeping. They are calling you, Waris Shah!'

It is a beautiful, moving poem, and also the famous Urdu writers, Krishan Chander and Saadat Hassan Manto, beautifully wrote about the tragedy of Punjab, which suffered the most at that time – particularly Krishan Chander's[35] novel, *Ham Vahshi Hain* (We are Savages) and Manto's *Toba Tek Singh* and other stories.[36]

Partition of Punjab in 1947

Before Partition Hindus, Muslims and Sikhs were living side by side. There were no problems. There were mosques in Nawanshahr before Partition. There was also a Jain temple in Nawanshahr. The Jains were mostly traders. The Jains were very much in the minority – there were just a few houses. They were regarded as Hindus. Everybody was very amicable. We used to go to the Jain temple.

After 1947, when there was a lot of fighting and killing, a lot of Muslims from these districts went to Pakistan. There were political parties – the Muslim League and the Congress. People knew that the Muslim League wanted Pakistan and the Congress party wanted independence of a United India. Hindus, Muslims and Sikhs were killing each other in both parts of the country – in Pakistan and in India. The Sikhs suffered a lot in Pakistan, as did the Hindus. It was mostly the Hindus and Sikhs who left Pakistan and came to India. The Sikhs lost their most respected and holy place, Nankana Sahib.[37]

The Viceroy had a lot of talks with national leaders: Lord Mountbatten came. The Muslim League was adamant about having Pakistan, while Congress was for a secular, united India. It was the irony of history that India was divided into Pakistan and India. I still remember Nehru's 'tryst with destiny' speech. He said to one of his friends that it was like cutting off our head in order to cure a headache.

II   The Life Story of Mr Ram Krishan (Prashar)

Then I saw the Partition between Pakistan and India happening. People were killing all over the place. In [Indian] Punjab Hindus were killing Muslims and Muslims [were killing Hindus and Sikhs] in Pakistan. I saw our friends leaving their home and going to Pakistan. I remember a village near about Nawanshahr, when Muslims were attacked, all their womenfolk jumped in the well and died. We felt sorry for the people and we used to listen to Gandhi's appeal that 'this is bad, it should not happen, we should live together.' But it happened. It was a great tragedy.

I saw that with my friends. My Muslim friends who were studying at school were leaving and going to Pakistan and our Hindus and Sikhs from across the border were coming without anything. They were really bad days. When the refugees came, we used to deliver clothes and medicines in the villages nearby. [There was a] government relief camp. We used to go there and help in the distribution process. With the relief centres loads of refugees came to our village and some of them settled. My niece has told me something my sister Satyabhama remembers about our mother. People were lying injured in the streets outside our city. Neighbours were running around shouting 'rich pickings!' and taking gold ornaments from injured people. They were going looking, and they said, 'Come!' Our mother said, 'I don't want to see any of this. I don't want my children to see this. I don't want any part in this. It's not right.' She said, '*Change lukke gharan vich gunde laran maidan.*' [Good people are hiding in their houses, the vagabonds are on the battlefield.]

One of our relatives, my Mamaji [mother's brother] was living in Santnagar in Lahore. He was in the railway and, after retirement, he built a beautiful house in Santnagar, Lahore, and we attended his son's marriage, before Partition, in Lahore. The house was very nice. It was a three-storey building. He lost it all and came with his sons and daughters to India, empty-handed.

[The] same sort of stories we were hearing from [the] other side – Pakistan. There was only one man at that time who was trying very hard to stop the madness. He was Gandhi. [On the] 15th August 1947, when India and Pakistan were celebrating their independence, he was in Noakhali telling people not to kill each other.

Even before that, when [the] Muslim League started [a] direct action day in Calcutta, and there were a lot of casualties, Gandhi went to Calcutta and went on [a] fast unto death, and the killing was stopped. Lord Mountbatten praised him wholeheartedly and it showed his [Gandhi's] spiritual power over the people and showed India he was still a mass leader. But then, 30th January 1948, Nathuram Godse shot him, India wept and the world was stunned.

I remember nobody in our house had any food on that night. In my *mohalla*, when I related that news to the people, they all were sad. Some of them were crying. [I was the one who told them the news] because for years it was my routine to go to the bazaar, listen to the 9 o'clock news, come back, and tell the news to my *mohallewale* [people of the

II The Life Story of Mr Ram Krishan (Prashar)

neighbourhood] and on that day I did the same.

I attended the funeral march the next day in my town and I also heard Nehru's speech. He was really crying. I still rememder one of his phrases in the speech. He said, 'Light has gone, but I think I am wrong – that light will never go out. It will always be shining in our hearts.'

When Gandhi died there was a condolence meeting in our school and the head of [the] Hindi and Sanskrit department announced, 'I request Ram Krishan to prepare an essay on Gandhiji from Arya Kumar Sabha, [the] student wing of Arya Samaj.' Although I was not a member of Arya Kumar Sabha, I was very happy to [hear] that request and I remember that I wrote a brilliant essay on Gandhiji which started with a quotation from the great scientist Einstein. He wrote, 'The generation which has not been born yet will hardly believe that such a man ever walked on this earth in flesh and blood.' That essay was very much praised.

Also I [half] remember [the] great Hindi poet Dinkar's following verse:

bhago bhago nagraj
shunya men ja bhago, bapu yah
bhage jate hain
pakaro, pakaro, ... pakaro
we donon charan
dasta jinke sevan se chhuti pakaro
we donon pad jinse azadi ki ganga phuti,
lauto chhune do ek bar
phir apna charan abhayakari.
rone do pakar wahi chhati
jismen hamne goli mari.

O bearer of the earth, look, Gandhi is going away, away. You run, catch him, catch him. Hold those feet by which we gained independence and slavery was removed. Come to us. Let us touch your feet, which made us fearless. Let us cry. Let us hold your chest, the chest which we shot.

[To quote from *Mission with Mountbatten*, one of my favourite books][38] 'I was particularly impressed with the *Hindusthan Standard*... leader page... paragraph... "Gandhiji has been killed by his own people for whose redemption he lived. This second crucifixion in the history of the world has been enacted on a Friday – the same day Jesus was done to death one thousand nine hundred and fifteen years ago. Father, forgive us."' 'Among the phrases and thoughts that have remained in my mind was Sarojini Naidu's[39] assertion "It is therefore right and appropriate that he died in the City of Kings" and her dramatic plea, "My father, do not rest. Do not allow us to rest. Keep us to our pledge".'[40]

II   The Life Story of Mr Ram Krishan (Prashar)

On 15 December 1950 Sardar [Vallabhbhai] Patel died. Many in India believed that if he [had] been the first Prime Minister of India things would have been very different – [the] Kashmir problem would have been solved. He was Deputy Prime Minister of India and a great soldier of India's independence movement. He was [the] Bismarck of India, making India from the 562 states of British India. People loved him very much. The public meeting was called in Nawanshahr to mourn his death and I was really surprised when the people decided that I should preside [over] that. The night before, I wrote my address which I delivered and it was praised by various people in Nawanshahr.

4   My higher education and departure to England in 1954

After Mr Krishan went to DAV (Dayanand Anglo Vernacular) College, Jalandhar, he decided to move to England in 1954. He describes his experiences thus:

My higher education

I studied there up until what they called matriculation. It was conducted throughout the province and you need[ed] to pass to go to university. I passed the matriculation. It would be 1947–8.

From sixth to tenth class my friendship began with Raj Kumar Sharada. His father had a commission shop called Sakhichand Amarnath. [Another friend was] Satya Varat Bhuchar, whose house was mentioned in Nawanshahr's *Geographia* [a guide book] as a beautiful house, an important building of Nawanshahr. They belonged to a very rich family. We used to talk and play with each other and used to go to each other's houses.

I used to attend Arya Kumar Sabha and also had [an] interest in Congress rallies. So, as we reached tenth class we knew a lot about Indian politics and also important personalities in the local Congress committee. There was also Shakti Kumar's ayurvedic shop and I used to go daily there to read the newspaper, and I used to have a long discussion with him. People in the local branch of [the] Congress Party also knew me.

After that I went to college. I was a student of DAV College, Jalandhar and started studying in FA (Faculty of Arts). It was about 50 miles away from my town. The usual subjects were Sanskrit and Hindi, political science, economics, maths and so on. Sanskrit was my favourite subject. English was compulsory. My life at college was very good. I was living in a hostel which was in the college grounds and paying the fees for my education. We used to live in the boarding house and in the summer holidays come to Nawanshahr. Raj Kumar Sharada and Sata Varat Bhuchar were with me.

The professors who used to teach us were very good. They wanted to give us a good education and all the facilities of a modern college were available there and a lot of people passed their exams with distinctions. I am talking now about 1951/52 when things were calm again. People were studying hard and there was law and order. There were no problems and it was a very good life I would say – many good friends. We used to go to cricket and football matches, and there were the Students Union and politics. I passed my FA and wanted to continue my study to BA, but my friend Raj Kumar Sharada failed, so I waited for a year so that he [could take a] complementary examination [i.e. resit] and so we could join together to study the BA course.

In Nawanshahr the Radhakrishnan Arya College opened in 1952. I was there when Nehru laid the foundation stone. I joined the college to do my BA course and I took Political Science along with other subjects, Hindi and Sanskrit. When I look back to my years in college, those were the golden years of my life. As I said before, I was very interested in Hindi literature, I was the editor of the Hindi section of the college magazine and the editor was our professor of Hindi. I said to him, 'Well, the magazine is ready, why don't you write the editorial?' He said, 'No, you are very good, you write the editorial.' And I wrote the editorial. He said, 'Brilliant editorial!' It was a comment on prevailing literary trends in Hindi literature, because I was immersed in who is writing what in Hindi and used to read all the Hindi writers in those days. Also, Mr Shakti Kumar Vaid was very respected in literary circles. He also praised my editorial. He said, 'Very mature.'

At that time we made something of a forum and I think, if I remember, we called it Nagar Sudhar Kameti (City Reform Committee). They selected me as general secretary and I was very active in that and I remember it attracted all the councillors of the municipal committees. We used to put proposals to improve the city's welfare.

In [the] summer holidays I think I went to Delhi because I heard that Harivansh Rai Bachchan[41] [was] coming to attend that *kavi sammelan* (poetic conference), along with three other prominent Hindi poets, and it was chaired by Pandit Banarsidas Chaturvedi.[42] He was a member of Rajya Sabha (i. e. upper house of parliament). I was very happy when I heard Bachchanji reciting his 'Madhushala'. [On the] second or third day I attended another function, which was presided [over] by the then Prime Minister, Lal Bahadur Shastri. I enjoyed the proceedings of that conference which was attended by many renowned Hindi writers and scholars.

There was another function I attended – that was a reception [for] Acharya Kishoridas Bajpai. He was a famous grammarian, a great writer, and there I met Sri Janinder Kumar, [a] great Hindi novelist, great Gandhian scholar, [a] thinker) and their speeches really thrilled me. So, I was thinking myself, 'One day I will be a writer in that category and my fame will be everywhere in the Hindi world.' There in Nawanshahr, in my college, [the] Professor of Hindi and Sanskrit was saying to me, 'In [the] MA we guarantee that you will be first in Punjab and other surrounding provinces,' and [he] always insisted that I write and [he said], 'One day that will be published in Hindi literary journals.'

Deciding to move to England

So, that was the castle I was building in the air. The night came when it all shattered. It

II   The Life Story of Mr Ram Krishan (Prashar)

was about midnight when I woke up with [hearing] my mother's slow sad talk to my father. I heard my father saying to Mum, 'What's the matter? Why you are weeping?' She said nothing. Father said, 'Don't worry. Everything will be all right.' Then she said, 'What are you going to do?' Father said, 'I will write to Chhota Babu in Calcutta.' I was listening [to] all that, and when Father said that I at once realised that Chhota Babu must have sacked my father from the job – because he [Chhota Babu] was [the] new boss of Thakurdas Sureka Limited. Then Father said, 'I had his letter and he said that you can stay in Nawanshahr, and no need for you to come to Calcutta for your service.' So mother kept crying.

In the morning, when I got up, everything seemed normal. My mum was silent, doing all the household work, as she always used to do, preparing food. My father was replying to a letter which he [had] received from the boss. After finishing the letter, he gave me the envelope and said, 'Go and post it.' That was always my duty: whatever letters he used to write, he used to give to me, and I went to the Post Office and put [them] in the letter box. On my way to [the] Post Office there was a lonely place to sit down. I sat down and cleverly opened the envelope and read it. It was [a] begging letter. Father wrote, I still remember, 'I have received your letter. You tell me, at this age, with my children, where shall I go? Without money, how can I carry [out] my *grihasthi* [i.e. family responsibilities as father and husband]? If I have done anything wrong, when I come to Calcutta you should have told me. I request you to consider your decision and please reply what you want [me to do]. [At] this age, how can I do any new job? The best part of my life I have served you. So please reply soon.' I read it and posted the letter.

I said to myself, 'Ram, that's it! *Ab udja re panchi, yeh desh hua virana.*' [i.e.] 'Now, bird, fly away!' 'This country is now foreign to you.' I thought that I should stop all this castle-building and see the situation. It was like being thrown from sky to earth. I didn't know what to do. If the household situation is this, what is going to happen? I prayed to God 'Let this not happen for a bit.' But I decided that soon I should be thinking of becoming an earning hand for the family. But how? It was a big question. Something in my heart was saying to me that [the] boss will agree to my father's request. Why? I didn't know. But it was nearly ninety per cent. I was convinced it will not happen. I can't give any reason for that feeling.

After five days the postman came and I was outside the house and he said, 'That's a letter for your father.' He always used to give the letters to me and I used to give [them] to Father. When I had that letter in my hand I was one hundred per cent sure that it was not a negative letter. Father opened the letter, read it very calmly, quietly; he said to my mother, 'Get ready. We are going to the temple,' and he also said [this] to me. It was afternoon and we went to the nearby temple, and we all prayed, and he said, 'Babu said, "All right, you can come and join your service."' We all were very happy and thanked God for that.

After Father went to Calcutta Mother never said anything to me at all but I knew what

II   The Life Story of Mr Ram Krishan (Prashar)

happened and was determined that something I must do to lighten the burden of my father. Soon the things became normal. The money was coming from Calcutta.

We were looking for a job after college finished. Raj Kumar Sharada [was], one of my very good friends and we were like twin brothers), [and] his brother, Hari Om Sharada, said that we should go to England because at that time many people were going to England. (Hari Om's family had a shop in Nawanshahr called Bata Shoe Company.) His brother-in-law was living in Coventry, [in] Princess Street – they were already here. He said, 'They have a house here and you will go and live there and start.'

I thought about that and I said, 'No, I want to study on.' But Raj said, 'What are we going to do after finishing the study? Life of a clerk? What will you get?' etc. It was after the war and England wanted the manpower because their people were rebuilding after the war. I asked what we would do in England. He said that people are there and we are getting letters from them and my brother has heard that they are earning a lot of money there. He said we would go and we would earn the money and we'll send the money. I said, 'No, I don't want go to England' because I wanted to study. But I thought a lot about that. One of my professors said that I really shouldn't go, I should stay in Punjab and continue my studies as I would get very good marks. [However], I said my friend was going and I would go.

My father was in Calcutta. I wrote him and told him that I wanted to go to England with my friend. He knew my friend; I asked his opinion. He wrote me back saying, 'Look here I don't want that in the future you should say to me that you have done a very wrong thing by going to England. The decision will be yours. I want you to continue with your studies but you have got your own decision to make. You can never then blame me in the future if something goes wrong.' I was very much impressed by his answer. I wrote back to him saying that I wanted to go to England. He said that was 'All right if you want to go to England.' I thought for a day and I decided to go with my friend and posted a letter telling my father of my decision. After three days, [a] telegram came to me from my father, 'OK, go to England. Before going to England, meet me in Calcutta.'

We got passports: there was a passport office in Shimla in those days and [we] had to fill in an application form to the government of India that we wanted to go. After that the passport office granted us [our passports] because in 1954 not many people were coming. People were just starting to come.

So the day came when my mother packed my luggage. We were ready to catch the bus from Nawanshahr to Jalandhar and from there Hari Om Ji and Raj Kumar would have caught the train to Bombay and I went to Calcutta, and it was decided that they would meet me [at] Victoria Terminus (Bombay) [it (now Chhatrapati Shivaji Terminus) is the main railway station in Mumbai].

My mother and sister were downstairs, people of [the] *mohalla* were coming with [a] lit-

II The Life Story of Mr Ram Krishan (Prashar)

tle bit [of] *shagun* and giving [it] to my mother. My friend Satya Varat Bhuchar came to say goodbye [to me] downstairs and gave me a little present. That day I went on the flat roof of my house and I saw that big banyan tree in my *mohalla*. Beneath there was Lord Shiva's temple. I bowed my head to Lord Shiva, praying that my family should be hail and hearty. 'I am separating myself from them and I don't know when I will come back,' and [I] felt how the life is so harsh that I have to go.

My friend Satya Varat Bhuchar – he was crying – gave me a big hug and a little gift wrapped in paper. I was surprised when I saw my professor of Hindi standing outside. I said, 'What are you doing?' He said, 'I thought I must say goodbye to you and will accompany you both up to [the] bus station.' I was really honoured that [the] professor came to say me goodbye – very strange to me.

My sister, my mother, Professor Sahib, Raj and [I] all went to [the] bus station together, and suddenly a Hindi verse came to my mind which I recited in my heart, and that was:

chanchal man mat hore rahi
jana tujhko dur
jana to ghabrana ho re
nain kyon bharpur.

That means: O mind, don't become agitated. You are going to a faraway place. If you are going, why are you so upset? Why there are tears in your eyes?

[The] bus came – Hari Om, Raj Kumar [and I] rode in the bus and said goodbye to all, so Nawanshahr disappeared in a few seconds.

I went to Calcutta and met my father and his boss, who begged me to stay [in India] and he was quite prepared to give me a monthly salary to work in his firm. Surprisingly, I remember my father saying to him, 'Well, Chhote Babu, he will not serve in your firm. He has decided to go to England', and that was that.

When I reached Bombay, after a few days I opened the gift which Satya Varat Bhuchar gave me. When I opened [it], there was *mitti* (clay, earth) in that and a note to me: 'Always think of India's earth. Never disgrace that.' I was overwhelmed and I told Raj, and Raj and [I], we were both in tears.

[In Bombay] my friend and I boarded a P&O ship Chusan. We boarded that ship and after two weeks we landed in Tilbury in England. We came by ship which was much cheaper than plane. It was a cruise ship so it was very nice. We were only allowed three pounds by the government. On board ship there was a library: I read Louis Fischer's story of Gandhi there. We met friends and people. We sometimes attended a dinner and dance. I enjoyed going [through] the Suez Canal, when the ship was very slow. Some [passengers] left the ship to see the pyramids and, after two days, they joined our ship.

II The Life Story of Mr Ram Krishan (Prashar)

As for food, there was vegetarian food, Indian food, rice, vegetables, ice cream, pudding and so on. We did not have English food. I attended many entertainment programmes on the ship. They used to show us a film: I watched the first Norman Wisdom film on that ship, 'Norman Wisdom in the Army'. On the ship they were very nice people. They showed us the biggest part of the ship, down to the Captain's rooms.

Many people on the ship were Indian. There were English people also, and various nationalities. I remember a lot of nurses were going from India to France to train as nurses.

I think on 6 November 1954 my friend Raj Kumar Sharada [and I] landed at Tilbury. From there we went to St Pancras station and then to Euston.

5 New life in Coventry: work and leisure, illness, discrimination

Mr Krishan came to Coventry in the UK in 1954 and started a new life. He recalls his memories thus:

My work and leisure in Coventry

From [Euston station] we landed [at] 20 Princess Street, Coventry. Hari Omji's relatives greeted us very warmly and we were puzzled at the weather at that time. It was dark everywhere, grey sky, the houses looked different from Indian houses – the roofs were not flat.

Both brothers took us to [the] pub in Coventry and gave [us] beer to drink, but we didn't have it because we were not drinking, and they were saying, 'You've come to England and have got to drink beer. It's the normal thing to do.'

I thought I should study journalism here. [However], at that time [as I have said] the Government of India only allowed [us] £3, so when I came here I realised that £3 was nothing. I wrote to the London School of Journalism saying that I wanted to study journalism. They said yes, but it was, I think, £300 a year, and that was impossible. We couldn't go back or our friends would mock us saying, 'They were going to England and now he has come back.'

At that time there was a custom among Punjabis that if you hadn't got a job, then rent and food expenses they used to bear, and they were relatives so they were not charging us. As soon as the chap got the job, on that day he was responsible for his rent, food and other expenses. The friends will say, 'From tomorrow, you should start looking for a job.' In the end we went to Alfred Herbert Limited,[43] and I remember that the foreman asked me a question: 'Do you understand English?' I replied, 'Yes, I can explain your thoughts, emotions and sentiments in very nice English.' So he was a bit surprised and gave me the form to fill up. I filled up the form.

II The Life Story of Mr Ram Krishan (Prashar)

Then my friend [and I] were sent to the foundry to work, and when I saw all of that I knew I could not do this type of work and I sighed heavily, 'O God, was I born to do that?' Within one or two days the foreman of the foundry said, 'He is not good, he can't work in the foundry,' so I was transferred to the machine shop. My friend stayed in the foundry – he was much stronger than me.

There was one Indian who started on the same day in the machine shop. We were given brooms to clean the floor and we didn't know what to do with them, because they were different [i.e. long-handled] from our brooms in India, so the foreman, Mr Wagstaff, came out of his office and glanced at us and said, 'Well, I will tell you how to use this broom.' No other foreman will try to do that, and he showed us how to use the broom. That's how we started our job. It was a labourer's job from 7.30 to 4.30, and Saturday used to be overtime.

In the foundry money was a bit higher than [in the] machine shop, but I was happy with my job, because it was light work, cleaning the floor. There was a tray where all the gang put their cups and my job was to fill those cups with hot water and give the cups to them, and then they used to work on the machine, and while they were working they used to drink tea and eat sandwiches. An hour used to be dinner time, from 12 to one. At that time, some used to go to the canteen, others used to eat their sandwiches.

It was a very isolated life. There were Indian people who owned the house and we were paying rent and we were living there. That was a house where 10 people used to live. Two rooms upstairs and two downstairs. I remember ten shillings [50p] a week was the rent and it was very crowded. There was not much Indian food available at that time – I am talking about 1954. Butter was [still] rationed.[44] Life was quite tough, going to work and coming back, going to work and coming back.

When we came in 1954 there was no central heating, but there was a coal fire. Five or six people used to live in one room. [Unlike many houses at that time] there was a toilet inside the house in Princess Street. In Coventry there were public baths. People used them, or they used to have a bath in their houses, a [tin bath] tub, but mostly people went to the public bath. Of course there were no [fitted] baths in the houses. Once a week we used to take a bath in Livingstone Street in Coventry. They used to [run] hot and cold water [to fill the bath] and we paid [an extra] half a crown (two shillings and six pence) – it was a lot of money in those days, like a bribe – and the caretaker used to give us [the] key. Then we [could] have a bath and [pull the plug out] so that [the] dirty water should go away [and] we could have a fresh bath. It was in the 1960s when the government gave the grant that you could have a bath in your houses. It made things a lot easier.

[There was] flour for chapattis [which] we used to buy from the shop. Cauliflowers and potatoes and all these things were easily available. Mostly we used to have lentils/*dal*, potatoes, cauliflower, and in turn we used to cook the food, and in the night we used to have the meal. We were all working different shifts.

After starting work in Alfred Herbert Limited I collected all [my] wages for a month and sent all the wages to my father in Calcutta. I wrote in my letter, 'This being the first salary of my life, some of that money you should, as you wish, use in some religious act at the temple.' He was very pleased and he said, 'I showed your letter to all my friends and they were praising you [saying], "You are very lucky to have such a son."'

A lot of people were working in the foundries. There were big foundries in Coventry [and companies like] Dunlop and G.E.C., Jaguar etc. There was plenty of work here in Coventry: people got jobs easily for what hours they wanted. My wages were very low. It was £8 a week – that meant you got £24 for three weeks – but on the fourth week the total was £40. (At that time £1 was equal to about 13 rupees.) That money was very good because food prices were low, and you had nothing to spend it on apart from shoes and clothes. There were no pictures to see. You couldn't go out.

That is why I said we used to go to work and come back and save money. Our standard of living was comfortable. We only used to pay for our rent and food – lentils or cauliflower or whatever. I used to go to [the] pub. Some friends would come but we [didn't] drink. Mostly even now I don't. There were other people who used to go to the pub and they used to spend that money. They were working in the foundry and earned more than me.

Things changed. Later on people saved their money and used it to buy the house. After [wards] people started coming with their wives and children. Television followed: in the 1960s there were a lot of televisions. Fridges and central heating came a lot later on. Then they wanted central heating, televisions and cars: things were changing. There used to be a black and white TV in the food shop. In our house the landlord had a TV and we all used to go and watch it, but people were not interested in watching TV because you [would] get up in the morning at five or six o'clock, have a wash and go to work. In the evening we used to come from work, we used to wash our feet and be fresh, then [we] used to cook in the kitchen, eat our food. Nobody was there to prepare our food.

Coventry [had been] very badly hit during the war [including the destruction of Coventry cathedral in November 1940] [45] but then the picture was changing. There were new shopping centres, a new market place and the new Coventry cathedral was born [in 1962].

After some time some cinemas were showing Indian films in Leicester, Birmingham and other places. Then at the same time Indian shops were beginning to open in Coventry – Indian shops which used to sell the Indian stuff: *dal*, *chawal* [rice], *masale* [spices], *ata* [flour]. That would be in about 1955/56. A Sindhi [46] man [ran] one Indian shop. He used to come to the house and deliver the food and the rations. You could have flour, you

II The Life Story of Mr Ram Krishan (Prashar)

could have lentils, you could have tinned stuffs. Then in Leicester a lot of Indian shops started opening and then also there was a van full of food which used to come to Coventry from Leicester. They were delivering food to the different houses before the shops were opened. Then they disappeared when the shops opened [in Coventry].

What is interesting to me [is] that our generation who came said they would only spend five years here. 'We will earn the money and then we will go back to India.' But those five years never came because things were changing in India. There was such corruption: to get a job teaching you had to bribe. Then, when [you] see what we were having: there was free milk for the children, free education [and] the National Health Service. All these benefits were not in India at that time. Not even now, I think. So a lot of families were coming because life was comfortable in England.

We were sending money to our families so that was a good thing, and [our] parents said, 'When you are in a strong position, come back and marry.' Lots of people were doing this. My brother also studied and when he was in a job, that was the proper time to marry.

My illness

I was working at Alfred Herbert Limited. One day a government circular came [saying] that all the employees will be X-rayed, so I was also X-rayed with all [the] others. They found out that I'd got TB [tuberculosis]. I was very worried and the employers sent me to see the doctor. He examined me. I told him that I was vegetarian and he said, 'Look, I [will] send you to a hospital. You will be there for six months and will be OK.' Meanwhile I wrote a letter to my father, telling all this story. Surprisingly, his reply came that, for health reasons, there is no harm eating the meat.

I was admitted in [the] TB sanitorium near Hatton Village and was there for three or four months. My illness was not so grave, I never required an operation: with medicine and good food I was cured. I still remember I was admitted on Christmas Eve and the fellow asked me, 'What would you like to drink tomorrow?' I was surprised. I said, 'I don't drink.' He said, 'All right, we'll give you orange juice.' He said, 'As it is Christmas, tomorrow we are busy in a bit of festivity for the patients. That's why I asked you.' When I got up I saw the atmosphere of festivity – patients having coloured hats on their heads, and I was surprised to find a little gift by my bed, given by Santa Claus. It was a package of writing paper and a pen. That was the first Christmas present of my life.

Doctors, nurses, matron, they all were friendly. I remember writing a letter to [the] Indian High Commission in London [saying] that, as I am in hospital, I can't find any books in Hindi. After a week a very good parcel came. It was *Ajkal*, [a] Hindi magazine, published by [the] Government of India, and about five or seven books.

Matron used to take all of us for a walk on Sunday. It was nice and pleasant – green fields – up to Hatton Canal. I really enjoyed all that. I used to serve tea and coffee, Oxo, chocolate drinks to my fellow patients. Some of them became my friend – there was one teacher who was very friendly with me and after – when I was discharged from hospital – he invited me to his house in Cheylesmore. After so many years I now live in Cheylesmore!

When the date of discharge was coming they gave me the instruction: eating my food regularly at home. I told them that where I am living there is not any arrangement [for] that. So, when the doctor came, they told him and requested that a temporary arrangement should be made for me. He said, 'You can live another three weeks in the barracks' (from the war days, now used as temporary accommodation for the hospital).

I was very happy and stayed there, and then my friends came and I went home and started the job in Alfred Herbert Limited. My sick money was coming [while I was ill] and also, as I was a member of [the] Saturday Hospital Fund (which was run by the Unions), their benefit also came to me, so I saved a substantial sum.

Colour Bar: racial discrimination

There was discrimination at work. English people wanted us to work at a lower level. You started work as a labourer and after that [you might become] a storekeeper. Hardly anybody [from our community] worked on the machine. After a long time people went to the higher level. I can remember when I was working my foreman came to see me. He said, 'I am going to give you a bit better job.' There [was] labouring and there was another job which was a bit superior. So he said he would arrange it and I went for the job... After that I heard English men were going to strike. Why should a black man have that job? He withdrew the job. That was my experience of racial discrimination. In the services [too] there was racial discrimination.

We were interested in earning the money and sending it home, [and also] saving so that we could buy the house. Where we were living we were paying rent, so after some time we used to go and look and put a deposit on a house. I can remember an incident. I wanted [a] house and it was being advertised in the paper. I ran to the estate agent and said that I wanted this house. He said that I couldn't have it. He said, 'Don't take me wrong, but the owner of the house does not want to sell it to a black man.'

I was a black man! I didn't make a fuss because from very early childhood I was looking to the people who were poor in India, living on the streets in Calcutta, sleeping on the roads and I know how they were treated. I think you have heard of the untouchable people in India? I was not supporting... but I was looking at how he felt when he refused to sell. That was a bad thing and this is also a bad thing but anyway, as I said, we had the money and we got another house.

There was a colour bar: there was a working men's club in Coventry, but although it was

II   The Life Story of Mr Ram Krishan (Prashar)

a working men's club they never allowed the black or coloured people to join, sit down and have a drink. Even in the working men's club there was discrimination. The Indian Workers' Association (see p. 47) was against it – many people were against it. These things applied even in the public houses: our people were refused entry. The Indian Workers Association took them to Court. They lost [the case] because at that time there was no Race Relations Act.[47]

It was a very tough life. At [that] time there were English people who didn't like Asians or black people and who would tell Indian and black people that we couldn't live in their houses. We couldn't rent. There was quite a lot of racial discrimination.

There were Pakistani and other people, but mostly [Indian] Punjabi people and some Gujarati people where I used to work. There was a shop steward from Fiji island, but he was also Indian. After the Second World War England wanted manpower and a lot of immigrants came from India, Pakistan, Jamaica and other countries, and they were filling the unskilled jobs – bus drivers, bus conductors, unskilled jobs in factories, foundries… After some time Indian corner shops appeared which were highly appreciated by the people.

In Coventry (unlike some places) no black people and Asians were employed on the buses. There was a shop steward called Rajmal Singh [the Fijian Indian mentioned above]. He complained about that. There was a long struggle and in the end they agreed. We staged a campaign and I was also with them. I remember Mohan Singh – he was the first Asian bus conductor. There was racial discrimination all around. After some time, all our people [were] bus conductors or drivers or in the Council House. There have been two [actually, three] Asian Lord Mayors of Coventry, so it is very good.

When Harold Wilson (1916–1995, a British Labour Party politician, the Prime Minister [1964–1970, 1974–1976]) became Prime Minister of Britain the Race Relations Act was passed. The working men's clubs and the pubs couldn't do anything. They had to concede, otherwise it was illegal. That law helped us a lot. People also helped – many white people in the Labour Party, the Conservative Party and the Liberal Party. Especially the Labour Party was much more aggressive on that issue. The trade unions also helped very much. They were all against racial discrimination, gradually it was disappearing.

I remember Enoch Powell's speech[48] which was very bad. He made his infamous speech about rivers of blood. It created a lot of trouble. The country was in an uproar. There was a lot of opposition against him in all the parties. His own party, the Tory Party, expelled him. He left the Party and joined the Unionists in Ireland.

Society has changed. I am talking about [the 1960s and 1970s] when all this was happening. Asian society has also changed. People have become chartered accountants and doctors in society. Rich men own factories. A lot of things have happened. There may be some racial discrimination and colour bar, but I don't think it is so visible. Now you can go to clubs and pubs. They don't look at the colour of your skin and say that you are not eligible because you are Asian. It is a good thing.

6 The Indian Workers' Association (IWA) [49] and the Indian Cultural and Welfare Society (ICWS) [50]

Mr Krishan was involved in the Indian Workers' Association and the Indian Cultural and Welfare Society after he started to live in Coventry. This is how he describes them.

The Indian Workers' Association

I knew of the Indian Workers' Association and I attended their meetings. Mr. Rajmal Singh was President. Many other people were there. They were quite a good agitating body: they were against racial discrimination, they fought against job discrimination. They were very dedicated: they used to have a delegation to go to London to meet the [visiting] Indian political leaders when they came here to tell them of their affairs – how we [were] living here and what our grievances [were]. The Indian leaders always used to say, 'You are Indian but you should be loyal to this country also and join the progressive element of this country.' They were doing a good job.

They [the members of the Indian Workers' Association] were very vocal in local affairs about racial discrimination. They would also indulge in social affairs; one of their branches would show Indian films. There were also other associations. We sometimes used to be [in] competition [with each other] and we would wind each other [up] a bit, but not much. After some time I finished with the Indian Workers' Association [and now] I don't hear any more about the Indian Workers' Association. Once upon a time they were quite powerful, quite vocal and they did a good job for the people of Coventry.

Trade unionists were there [like] Mr. Rajmal Singh. Once there was some kind of disease in Coventry – smallpox? Some of the English people in the English shops used to refuse to take [our] clothes for dry cleaning or in the washing machines which they used to put in the shops. There were shops where Indians used to take their clothes so that they could be washed. The owners said no, because they thought this was a disease and they might be infected. Rajmal campaigned against this and, after some time, he was successful.

Our people [had] their own political parties. We were [also] very much attracted to the Labour Party and the trade unions. We were seeing how democratic the country was. Churchill was very popular in wartime, but his party was thrown out after the war and, after some time, Sir Anthony Eden (1897–1977, a British Conservative politician) became Prime Minister (1955–1957). I remember Gamal Abel Nasser (1918–1970; the second president of Egypt, 1956–1970) in Egypt, when he nationalised the Suez Canal, and there was quite an uproar here; how Britain and France went to war and how they were

II The Life Story of Mr Ram Krishan (Prashar)

The ICW's reception for Vyjayanthimala in the Savoy Theatre, Coventry.

defeated. Then Anthony Eden had to resign. That is how democracy worked.

The Indian Cultural and Welfare Society

[As I've said] we used to attend the meetings of the Indian Workers' Association, but somehow we didn't like their ideas. There were about five or six of us wanting somewhere to go together. We were all well-educated; we were thinking of putting an end to the boredom of life. Some of our Punjabi friends said that we should do something and we made a collective decision to start a library. We got Punjabi literature from India [and] Hindi newspapers. We contacted a Hindi publisher and they started to send a lot of the material free, and we used to pass it on to our friends and they used to read that. We sent a year's subscription to a popular Urdu newspaper, *Partap*. A lot of people were Urdu-speaking, and they were very pleased. People used to come between 4 and 5 on Saturday and Sunday and [they] used to [learn] what was happening in India. That is what we were doing and people were very happy.

A lot of people from Punjab were working in foundries and in various other jobs and on Sunday they used to come to our house (as they were not very educated) and they would say, 'Please write a letter to my wife' because they didn't know how to. We would write the letters for them: 'I am sending so much money…' What I am indicating is that we started a kind of service for them, typing the letters. Somebody would come with a form and we would fill the forms in. We also used to give advice to needy people.

From that we started an Indian Cultural and Welfare Society in 1958/59. A constitution was approved and the executive committee thought that we should show Indian films to the public. We arranged Indian films. We used to hire them from London and show them in Coventry so people were having that kind of entertainment. That was done step by step. There was a gentleman called Mr Pochi and he arranged Indian films to send us and charge [a] reasonable fee.

People were pleased because there was not so much entertainment for Asian people in Coventry in those days. On Saturday we used to write a poster informing the people that

II The Life Story of Mr Ram Krishan (Prashar)

this kind of film will be showing on Sunday. We arranged to have visits from film stars visiting, which was very popular. I remember arranging a visit for Shyama (a popular Punjabi actress), Shashi Kala (famous from [the] film *Gumrah*, Sohrab Modi (who directed the famous film *Jhansi ki Rani*) etc. [Our society] became very popular due to the Indian films. That was what we were doing.

The most memorable thing we did was Vyjayanthimala's visit to Coventry.[51] Vyjayanthimala Bali [came] to do a performance in a Coventry theatre and people came from Leicester and Nottingham to see her performance. When we met [Vyjayanthimala] we were thrilled. She was a very humble lady. She came with her grandmother. We arranged a reception at [the] Savoy Theatre [in] Radford for her where we presented Indian savoury pakoras, samosas etc to her. Seeing these she was very surprised and she was overwhelmed with joy – she said that she was not aware that all these things [like samosas] were available here in England. She came from Paris; she was the head of a goodwill mission to Europe supported by the Indian government. In 1958/59 there was no chance of [Indian food] in Paris. When we had the samosas she started eating with her hands [and] we were very surprised to see her humbleness. She said she did not have any makeup so she [could] not perform. Somebody's youngest daughter went to the shop and brought all the makeup for Vyjayanthimala. She was a very good dancer, and after the show she was sitting and talking with us all. Our image of the actors and actresses vanished!

We started a free bus on Sunday and arranged selected bus stops from where people [could] ride free on the bus and come straight to [the] Savoy Theatre where we used to show Indian films. There [were] no charges for unemployed people and students [to see the films]. This step created a stir in Coventry and was very popular and affected our competitor, [the] Indian Workers' Association, which was showing Indian films in the Ritz.

Mr Cresswell, an ex-Lord Mayor of Coventry, was the President of our society. We used to celebrate [the] Indian festival of Divali (Diwali), which was very much appreciated by our members and the Indian public.

7 Getting married

In 1964, almost ten years after Mr Krishan started to work in Coventry, he got married. He recalls his experiences thus:

My friend Raj Kumar Sharada and I went back to India because our parents wanted us to go back and get married. They were very pleased to see us. I saw, and Raj also saw, that our parents were old, and after some time our parents started looking for suitable girls for us.

Before we went to India, [a friend] Ram Swarup Kaushish [had] told us to meet his fa-

II The Life Story of Mr Ram Krishan (Prashar)

ther, Bhagat Ram, and tell him [he was] all right. [Bhagat Ram] was very famous in his village, [which was] called Bilga. So, after a few days, we went to see him in his village and I remember going with Raj and we were walking through green fields of mustard. It was bright winter sunshine and we were talking, about three or four miles away from the village. [We were saying] that he [Bhagat Ram] is a very smart man and – [from] whatever we have heard – he is robbing people, making false promises to fulfil their desires.

When we reached the village, a lad came from outside the house and he told us that his uncle [was] in his fields, so we went there. As soon as the old man saw us he stood up from the charpoy, welcomed us warmly and pointed [to] us to sit down on the nearby charpoy. We told him the whereabouts of his son [and] said he [was] doing well. We said to him, 'We have come to India so that our parents should arrange marriage[s] for us.' The gentleman pointed a finger to me and said, 'His marriage will take place very soon, but your friend's marriage will create problems. So he will postpone his departure (because he wanted to go to England with you).' [He continued, 'Half an hour ago you were calling me all sorts of things, saying insulting words against me and telling each other that I am robbing the people and a fraud.' His remarks fell like a bombshell and we were taken aback, and in [a] feeble voice I said, 'No, no, no, I…' and he cut me off saying, 'Don't tell lies. Weren't you [saying] all these things?' For a moment we felt that the earth should split and engulf us. But he said, 'Forget all that' and he talked nicely and called a boy, gave us tea, and talked about other things, and we were listening like guilty boys. He said, 'Well, you come and see me again, whenever you want.' We requested him to tell us our future. He said, 'I have already told you.' Anyway, as the months went by, his fortune telling was one hundred per cent true.

My father's former boss arranged a very big event in Benares, which is a holy city in India. It was the inauguration of the Tulsi Manas Mandir [an impressive temple that has the Ramayana inscribed on its walls inside] and Ratan Lal Surekha invited my father. He said he was too old, so I went in his place. I attended the event and, when it was finished, [Ratan Lal Surekha] called me and said, 'Are you taking off?' and I said, 'Yes, we are going,' and I thanked him for inviting us to the event. On the eve of my departure, Ratan Lal Surekha called me. He offered a lot of money to me, saying, 'No I am not giving it to you – you take this money to your father and tell him that with his hard work and wisdom that tiny firm is now a big firm – that is all due to his kind guidance and wisdom. This is in appreciation.' I am just telling you how much he respected my father. What an irony that the person who sacked my father just over ten years before and changed the direction of my life [was] now paying a tribute to my father's management and skill!

I got married on 28 February 1964 to Adesh Kanta, daughter of Mr Kartar Chand Rajp, who was a very respected man. He worked in Tanganyika and Kenya as a Permanent Railway Inspector. For his services he was awarded a British Empire medal by the present Queen. When Kenya became independent Mr K. C. Rajp was retired on a good pension and he, with all his family members, went to reside in Banga, about ten miles from Nawanshahr.

II The Life Story of Mr Ram Krishan (Prashar)

It happened that Raj [was] married to the girl from Delhi. His marriage [got into] trouble and he got [a] divorce. Then Mr Bhagat called me. He proposed the daughter of his friend who was [an] ex-*tahsildar* [revenue officer]. Then I told this to Tayaji (Raj's father) and Hari Omji. Both the families negotiated [with] each other and, after a while, the marriage was arranged with her and Raj got married.

[While] all this [was] happening, I met Sri Bhagat Ramji three or four times, and he was very pleased [with] whatever I [had] done to assist him [in arranging] [Raj's] marriage. I was married at that time and he said to me, when I was going to Nawanshahr, 'Come and meet me tomorrow afternoon.' The next day I went to his village and met him. He called me to his worship room, ordered me to sit down on a *gaddi* [large cushion] and closed his eyes, and after a minute [he] gave me an apple. He said, 'Take this apple. [In] the middle of the night, [at] 12 o'clock, wash this apple, eat half of the apple yourself and [the] other half, give [it to] your wife to eat, and rest assured that your first child will be [a] son.' I bowed my head to him and went back and did what he asked. He was one hundred per cent true to his words. When we came back the first child was a son.

After Raj's marriage he called Raj also, gave him an apple, and the same thing happened with Raj also. With our savings Raj and I had a house here [in Coventry] at 49 St. Patrick's Road which we rented [out]. It was a three-storey house. We were then in a strong position economically. What we [had done] Raj and I, before returning to India, [we had] left Coventry and [gone] to Loughborough – my sister and Raj's sister were living there – and we [had] bought a house there and started a grocery shop. When we got married we [planned that] we would come here.

[First, when we returned to Coventry after getting married] we came to 23 Aylesford Street and [we were] met by Raj Kumar's brothers. Then my wife's sister requested us to pay a visit to them in Langley, Birmingham. So I went there with my wife and spent about four or five months and Raju [Rajeev], my first child, a son, was born there in 1964. Meanwhile, Raj sold 23 Aylesford Street [and] went to Loughborough, and then we all went to Loughborough [and] started living there.

[However], after some time I realised that business was not so profitable that we (both families) could lead a comfortable life, so I decided to have a job in Coventry. After some time I [bought] a house, 63 Wyley Road [and] I started to work at Alfred Herbert Ltd Machine Tools again because I [had been] happy in my job. I was working as a storekeeper. My daughter Rajni was born in May 1966 [while we were living] at 63 Wyley Road and then Rita (Ritu) was born in May 1971.

Now my friend Raj was running [the] business in Loughborough and I was working at Alfred Herbert Machine Tools Limited in Coventry and every Friday I used to go to 49 St Patrick's Road to collect the rents from the tenants, because the whole house was rented [out]. My children [had] a nice childhood [in] Wyley Road [but], after some time, we felt that 63 Wyley Road [was] becoming [cramped] accommodation for the children.

II The Life Story of Mr Ram Krishan (Prashar)

As they were growing up they needed more rooms and we needed a big house. So, after a talk with my friend Raj, we settled that he should run the business in Loughborough (and he also had a residence in Loughborough, apart from the business premises) and I moved to 49 St. Patrick's Road, and we rented out the upper part, and the children were going to school. Raju went to Caludon Castle school and Rajni and Ritu went to the Church of England school in Cheylesmore. Rajni used to look after her brother and [her little] sister, taking her to school. Later on my friend disposed of the property and business in Loughborough and he went to Canada. That was the end of the friendship.

After some time I sensed that my marriage was having trouble, so we got a divorce. After that I had to sell the house in St. Patrick's Road and the money was divided between [my wife] and me. They were very bad days – very bitter days. I will leave it to my children to pass judgement on our divorce episode and the effects on them. At the present time my relations with my children and grandchildren are very cordial and I have no bitterness towards anybody. I think bitterness eats you.

Raju and Ritu went with their mother and Rajni very bravely stayed with me and we left Coventry and went to stay with my sister in Loughborough for six months. Then we came to Coventry. My friend, Mr Judge, had two houses so he rented 23 Dugdale Road to us and, after some time, we bought the house from him. I always term those my 'exile years'. I used to go to my mother-in-law, because my relations with my mother-in-law and sister-in-law were very cordial, friendly and respectful. They helped me a lot in those exile years. I remember with great gratitude the time I spent with Mama (my former mother-in-law).

Things here were becoming bad: Margaret Thatcher (a British Conservative politician) became Prime Minister [in 1979]. After that our life in England changed. She was a controversial leader in my opinion. At that time there was terrible unemployment. She put a poll tax which people opposed. Many things she did were unpopular for the working class people. It was a period of darkness in my opinion. She tamed the trade unions. Some people said the unions were doing wrong things. But that is a matter of opinion. Economically people were unemployed and companies went bankrupt. Industry was going down. There was a lot of unemployment. Our big firm, which was one of the largest machine tool firms, made me redundant. A lot of people were made redundant. Then this divorce business came. They were terrible days, but I survived.

Remarriage

[Many years later], I was sitting in my house and had a telephone call from the priest at the temple. He asked me to go to the temple. I asked what was the matter, and he said, 'There is a lady here and she wants to know about Hinduism, and you can explain.' They always used to call [me] – even now, if students come, then I go and [speak to] them. I said, 'OK.' When I arrived at the temple there was an English lady sitting there and she asked questions about Hinduism. I answered her questions. She was a soft-spoken lady, talking in Hindi; I was surprised to hear her talk. That was Eleanor!

My second wife, Eleanor, and I cutting our wedding cake, in our house in Coventry.

I thought it was very strange that she had so much knowledge of Hinduism. She then told me that she is a lecturer in Warwick university. She [had been] a teacher in India for three or four years. [Actually, Eleanor was in India September 1974 to March 1977]. She met me [next on] the bus and said that she wanted to learn Hindi. I said that I would come and see whether she could write Hindi. I went to her house and dictated some line in Hindi and she wrote it in Hindi. I said, 'Do Hindi O level.' I taught her and she passed O level in Hindi with a first class grade. I said that was very good and she could do A level. She [prepared] for A level and I was teaching her three days a week. She did her A level, I liked her and she also liked me and we married. I was so very happy and the children also liked her. My previous wife had also remarried. That is how destiny smiles sometimes.

8 Community organisations and interfaith relations in Coventry

For a very long time Mr Krishan has been a member of the Hindu Temple Society (Coventry), which is now at 380 Stoney Stanton Road. He was involved in other organisations. He recalls the history of those organisations thus:

The Hindu Temple Society (Coventry)

A lot of people came to Coventry – Hindus, Muslims and Sikhs and there were no places of worship. 274 Stoney Stanton Road was the residence of Mr Nagin Das Parekh before [the] Hindu Temple Society purchased this building, and the Hindu people gathered and started worshipping there. The first floor of the building was used by the Hindu Temple Society for daily prayers which we say to our deities. We started the celebration of festivals like Ramnavami, Divali etc. [The] Hindu Temple Society members were Punjabi and Gujarati Hindus. A lot of the old generation of Hindu Punjabis were members of the Society. In 1968 [the] Hindu Temple Society bought the house and then [in] 1977 to 1978, under the leadership of Mr R. P. Farmah, generated the donations which were used for construction of the main hall. I used to go to the temple.

In the beginning there were Gujaratis. Then something happened and the Gujaratis started their own Shree Krishna Temple on Stoney Stanton Road. I used to attend the

II   The Life Story of Mr Ram Krishan (Prashar)

The present Hindu Temple, Coventry.

executive committee, presided [over] by Mr P. K. Bhakri and, in those days, I remember Mr P. L. Joshi, Mr Nayar. They were very active in the committee.

Swami Satyamitranandji [52] and Morari Bapu [53] and the famous saints used to visit our temple and address the devotees. It was a lively place for Hindus. Unfortunately, there was a rift among the managing committee and some of them left us and started their own temple as [the] Sanatan Dharm Mandir in Mason Road. Before that, in the beginning, Arun Bhandari and [the] Hare Krishna people [54] were also with us. Later, they started their own temple in Kingfield Road, but we carried on.

In [the] old temple there was a priest, Mr Joshi; with his advice a women's wing of the Hindu Temple Society was also formed, called Janki Mandali Samiti. The first president was Sudarshan Bhakri, and they contributed a lot by encouraging women to come to the temple and take part in festivals. Every Tuesday they used to meet and [they] still do this, to recite *bhajan* and *kirtan* [i.e. to sing devotional songs] and also cook the food which is shared by everybody, without any distinction of caste and creed, and their activity is still continuing in 380 Stoney Stanton Road.

After some time we thought we should have a nice big temple. We purchased the land nearby at 380 Stoney Stanton Road, behind the petrol station, and the voluntary donations were building up and up. It took us a long time from 1977. The temple also bought a residential property. The day came when we opened a new, beautiful, purpose-built temple, after so many years, in January 2012 [with an] inauguration ceremony by the Lord Mayor.

The temple is open to all Hindus, but they are mainly from Punjab. People are very happy. Now the Gujaratis are coming [too] – all are coming. It is a very popular temple. Many devotees, when they visit the temple, praise the deities and say the *murti*s are wonderful. The *murti*s were carved in Jaipur, [55] India, which is famous for this purpose.

Our priest is a Gujarati. The rituals are [basically] the same whether a Hindu priest is from Punjab or Gujarat. They [Gujaratis] will have the same kind of rituals worshipping the gods and goddesses and the marriage and funeral ceremonies. We pray in Sanskrit and also in the local languages: Gujaratis praise the god and speak in Gujarati. Punjabis will speak Punjabi singing the glory of the goddess. The main worshipping ritual will be

II   The Life Story of Mr Ram Krishan (Prashar)

in Sanskrit [which] is used throughout [the] northern part of India by all the priests in whatever province they are – whether Gujarati or Punjabi or Maharashtrian or Bengali.

The temple [has] also got a very good relationship with the Sikh community in Coventry. P. K. Bhakri and I are members of the Indian Community Centre, which is mainly Sikh. Whenever a *nagar kirtan*'s procession goes through Coventry, the temple always honours them with tea, samosas, pakoras, honouring Vaisakhi.[56]

School children come [to the temple] and I tell them about Hinduism and the temple gives them refreshments and the temple is very popular among the schools. Also, many times, teachers' requests come and we always fulfil their request for students to visit the temple and learn about Hinduism.

The new temple was also visited by Swami Satyamitranandji and various saints, and in our capacity we serve the community. There are Hindi classes, yoga classes and *sanskar* classes [classes in correct Hindu conduct] conducted by the temple. (People come to learn mantras.) Once in a month, the library visits the temple and encourages people to borrow the Hindi and Gujarati books, because a lot of Gujaratis attend our temple.

When there was [the] Gujarat earthquake (it occured on the 26th January of 2001, India's 52nd Republic Day) many years ago, the temple collected money and we sent it. Recently, we collected over £3000 which we sent for the Nepal earthquake relief. We are very active in community affairs also. We called a meeting of various communities' representatives in our old temple, condemning the dowry-system.

Our president and executive committee and trustees serve the temple very nicely. On Dassehra Day a big statue of Ravan is erected and Ravan *dahan* (burning of Ravan)[57] is celebrated with great enthusiasm. Similarly, in [the] Divali celebration, sweets are distributed and the temple is illuminated.

As representatives from [the] Hindu Temple Society, I and Mr Banwari Lal [Sharma] attended the reception given by Her Majesty the queen and the Duke of Edinburgh in Buckingham Palace for her Golden Jubilee.

The events of 1984

In June 1984, the Golden Temple [in Amritsar, Punjab] was attacked. After that, on the 31st of October, Indira Gandhi was assassinated. I think there was bitterness for a time in those days. I still remember that, although [relations between] the Hindu community and the Sikh community were strained at that time, responsible people were saying, 'This happened in India and we read about it, [and] maybe sympathise about it. You can support or condemn according to your opinion, but we should not end the peace in Coventry.' Canon Peter Berry [from Coventry cathedral] called a meeting in the Chapel of Unity with all the Sikh and Hindu leaders and appealed for unity and peace and prayed

II The Life Story of Mr Ram Krishan (Prashar)

for all the people who were slaughtered in Punjab. There was a strain [locally], but eventually it went away.

When this kind of thing happens in India there is bound to be a reaction outside. We must keep cool heads, whether the news is good, bad or whatever. That is what happened in Coventry. There were radio talks. Hindu representatives were, according to their will, expressing opinions. There were never large-scale disturbances, like there were in India, because the British government was watching the situation. The British government were quite determined not to have a repetition of the things which were happening in India when the Sikhs were killed.

The Indian Community Centre

Hindus and Sikhs now have very good relations with each other. I am also a member of the Indian Community Centre – an executive member, a working committee member. It was formed a long time ago. We attend and we celebrate Diwali and Vaisakhi. They also have a very good place upstairs, very well decorated where marriages can take place in that room. They are mostly Sikhs because the Sikhs are in the majority here [among Indians in Coventry]. They also used to get a grant from the City Council of Coventry. Now they provide services – if somebody wants a passport or a visa they can go there for help. They can arrange the form, complete the form. A lot of people want advice. The Indian Community Centre also does that.

In Coventry [after the Christian community] the Muslims are [now] in the majority and then the Sikhs.[58] The Hindus are the third largest.[59] There was one bad incident many years ago when the British National Party[60] staged a procession. [In 1981] a Sikh boy [Satnam Singh Gill] was killed. There was uproar. Coventry was in a very tense state. [However], I will say mostly people are very nice – very happy. They do their jobs and the relationships are very good. It has always been a home for refugees. On the whole it is a very calm and peaceful city.

There was an International Youth Festival and people from Coventry came to our temple and we spoke with them. They were very much impressed and wrote us letters of thanks. This kind of thing is happening in this country with people visiting each other's places of worship and getting to know each other, and each of the religions. I think that is the best way to see how the other people are, what their beliefs are, and try to understand.

The Multi-Faith Forum

In Coventry [the Multi-Faith Forum] was an idea of the Bishop of Coventry, Simon Barrington-Ward in the late 1990s. As representatives [of the] Hindu Temple Society, Mr Ramesh Chandra Dhammi [and I], used to attend meetings in the then bishop's house. For a brief history of Coventry Multi-Faith Forum see Mehru Fitter's account in the ap-

II   The Life Story of Mr Ram Krishan (Prashar)

Harry Hall, the chairman of the Multi-Faith Forum with me, in front of symbols of world religions, 2015.

pendices. It was a good, noble idea, to join together to maintain racial peace and harmony. I am a trustee of [the Multi-Faith Forum].

We had the co-operation of the Lord Mayor and other civic dignitaries [in setting up a Peace Walk to take place in November], and it is still carrying on. My [memory is] that when we used to go on [the annual] Peace Walk, people were very happy to attend each other's religious activities. I remember one English lady saying to me, 'I never knew what is happening inside the walls of a Hindu temple or a mosque.' It created a lot of awareness for each other's religious activities.

Usually [the Peace Walk has been] led by the Lord Mayor of Coventry, also supported by Coventry Council, and general people. We [have] had a lot of students from Warwick University [and] Coventry University participating in our Peace Walk, going from the Chapel of Unity [in Coventry cathedral to the] mosque, Hindu temple, [and one year to a] Methodist church, [and another year to a] Spiritualist church and ending in [the] gurdwara, where we have our dinner. [The Peace Walk] [has

The walkers pausing near the ruins of the old cathedral.

become] popular and [it has been] reported in the *Coventry Telegraph* and in the Punjabi magazine *Desh Pardesh*.

I remember receiving a German delegation visiting our Multi Faith Centre. A university chaplain attends our meetings. Once we arranged the series of lectures about religions which locally have smaller numbers of followers – like Baha'i, Buddhist, Brahma Kumari, Jain, Quaker, Zoroastrian etc. Before that a series of lectures on Hinduism, Sikhism, Islam and Christianity was arranged by [the] Multi-Faith Forum which was well received. [The book] *Guru Nanak*, by local author [my wife] Eleanor Nesbitt and Gopinder Kaur was launched there, [at an event] which was inaugurated by the then Lord Mayor, Councillor Ram Lakha.

II The Life Story of Mr Ram Krishan (Prashar)

Many, many years ago, Revd Supriyo Mukherjee [and I] spoke on radio telling about [the] Multi Faith Forum's activity in the region.

9 Japan and Japanese culture

Mr Krishan is very interested in Japan and Japanese culture. This is how he describes it:

I first heard of Japan as a child from my father's library. I was reading a novel titled *Pariksha Guru* where a fellow who's Indian, living in India, in poor conditions, eventually visits Japan. He works very hard, spends many years in Japan, becomes a rich man and returns to India. And the character tells about [the] Japanese way of life, their habit of hard working and their attitude towards progressive life. Japan to my mind was a very advanced country when India was not independent. All Asia remembers when Japan defeated Russia [Russo-Japanese war, 1904–1905]. A wave of happiness went through Asian countries at that time and Asians were feeling proud of the fact that an Asian country can do that.

We also respect Japan and understand their feelings of shock and bewilderment when [the] atomic bomb was dropped in Hiroshima and Nagasaki (in August in 1945). At that time [as I have said already] I was in India and [I] remember India became very angry [about] this act of oppression. [The] general public condemned dropping the bomb. We respect Japan and call [it the] country of the rising sun. When they were in [the] Nuremberg trial, and the Japanese were declared criminals, our judge, an Indian, said, 'No.'

To the Japanese India is a sacred land. They respect Buddha and his teachings. So, for Indians, Japan is a valuable friend and guide. Japan is against the spread of nuclear weapons and, recently, in Coventry, on Hiroshima Day, I was happy to see the Japanese ambassador [attending] the Hiroshima Day [commemoration in the Chapel of Unity]. Hiroshima is a twin city [of Coventry]. I was delighted, too, at the end of 2015, to see on NDTV [New Delhi Television] Mr Shinzo Abe, the prime minister of Japan's visit to our holy city, Varanasi, where he was welcomed by the Indian prime minister, Narendra Modi, and was present for the *arati* ceremony by the river Ganga.

Eleanor and me with Mrs Hideko Okamoto in our living room in 2005 (photo by Professor Toru Okamoto, see page 14).

It is very odd that I read about Japan in a novel and then I had to leave Calcutta with

II The Life Story of Mr Ram Krishan (Prashar)

Eleanor and me with Professor Toru Okamoto in the Okamotos' flat at the University of Warwick in 2005 (photo by Mrs Hideko Okamoto, see page 14).

my family due to Japan – [the Indian] government [asking for the] evacuation of Calcutta, fearing Japan [would] bombard Calcutta. Then in August 1945 I became very agitated and angry [because of] the act of America [in] dropping [the] atom bomb on Japan, which I never thought they [would] do.

In 2004–2005 it was a great pleasure to meet Professor Toru Okamoto, who was in Eleanor's department at the university, and his wife, Mrs Hideko Okamoto. [Then], recently, meeting two Japanese [scholars] (Dr Maya Suzuki and Dr Hisae Komatsu) who visited our house, speaking in beautiful and idiomatic Hindi. [They are] working in Japanese universities, [one of them] teaching Hindi language to Japanese students. Last, but not least, Japanese students visiting our Hindu temple, and now meeting Professor Kiyotaka Sato who, knowingly or unknowingly, provides [a] coming generation of anthropologists [with] a lot of material on ethnic minorities in [the] Midlands.

10 Changing my passport

Mr Krishan has had two kinds of passport, an Indian one and a British one. He outlines his opinions thus:

There was always a delay at airports if you had Indian passports, then I realised that as I was living in England and my children were here it was better to have a British passport. As the years go by, India to my children will not be the same as for me.

If you live in a country, you should be loyal and respect their traditions and culture and live a good citizen's life according to their rules and regulations. I don't see any conflict, as England is a democratic country and whatever you think you can speak.

The photograph from my Indian passport, 1970.

II The Life Story of Mr Ram Krishan (Prashar)

Britain is a second home, and to our children it will be their first home. To an older generation India might be like a sacred land, but to our children it may be the holiday land.

Notes

1 Kolkata (Calcutta), the capital of the Indian state of West Bengal, is the principal commercial, cultural, and educational centre of East India. Previously known as Calcutta, the city changed its name in 1999 to the Bengali form, Kolkata. Its history dates back to around 1690, when an East India Company's factory was established in Kalikata, and Kolkata was born. See Maria Lord & Brian Bell, *Insight Guides: India*, London: Discovery Channel, 2004, pp. 221–229; K. Dutta & A. Desai, *Calcutta: A Cultural City*, Northampton: Interlink Books, 2008.
2 His name is Mr Ram Krishan. Prashar (spelled in various ways) is his family title which is used at the temple and the Indian Community Centre. Other members of his family use it as their surname. 'Bhakta' means devotee. His grandfather was a particularly religious devotee of mother goddess Durga, and so people used to call him Bhakta, Mr Ram Krishan's brother uses this surname and sometimes Mr Ram Krishan has used this name as well.
3 Marwaris are a trading and business caste originating from Marwar, the largest region of Rajasthan in India. They are predominantly Hindu, and also include a large number of Jains. See Medha M. Kudaisya, 'Marwari and Chettiar Merchants, 1850s–1950s: Comparative Trajectories', in Medha M. Kudaisya & Ng Chin-keong, *Chinese and Indian Business: Historical Antecedents*, Leiden: Brill, 2009, pp. 86–119; Tripathi, Dwijendra, 'From Community to Class: The Marwaris in a Historical Perspective', in B. L. Bhandai & Dwijendra Tripathi (eds), *Facets of a Marwar Historian*, Jaipur: Publication Scheme, 1996, pp. 189–196.
4 Jwalamukhi is a town in Kangra district in Himachal Pradesh in India. It has a famous temple to the goddess Jwalamukhi, the deity of the flaming mouth, for Hindu pilgrimage. See http://himachalhillstations.com/jawala-ji.html.
5 Bhagavad Gita, meaning 'Song of the Lord', is one of the holy books for Hindus. It has teaching said to be given by Lord Krishna. In the book, Krishna is talking to Arjuna, an archer, before the Kurukshetra War (also called the Mahabharata War) begins. See W. J. Johnson, *Oxford Dictionary of Hinduism*, Oxford: Oxford University Press, 2009, pp. 47–48; K. K. Klostermaier, *Hinduism: A Short History*, Oxford: Oneworld, 2000, p. 294; For the Bhagavad Gita, see Eknath Easwaran (introduced & translated), *The Bhagavad Gita* (Classics of Indian Spirituality), California: Nilgiri Press, 2nd edition, 2007.
6 Maharana Pratap Singh (1540–1597), a member of the Rajput (warrior) clan, the ruler of Mewar, a region in north-western India in the present-day state of Rajasthan. See Henry Scholberg (ed.), *The Biographical Dictionary of Greater India*, New Delhi: Promilla & Co., Publishers, 1998, pp. 82–84; Brishti Bandyopadhyay, *Maharana Pratap: Mewar's Rebel King*, New Delhi: Rupa Publications, 2007; Dr. Bhawan Singh Rana, *Maharana Pratap*, New Delhi: Diamond Pocket Books (P), Ltd, 2015.

7 Shivaji Bhonsle (c.1627/1630–1680), also known as Chhatrapati Shivaji Maharaj. An Indian warrior king and a member of the Bhonsle Maratha clan (a prominent group within the Maratha [warrior] clan system). See Jadunath Sarkar, *Shivaji and his Times*, Hyderabad: Orient BlackSwan, 1952 (fifth edition), 2015 (reprint); Surjit Mansingh, *Historical Dictionary of India*, New Delhi: Vision Books, 2000, pp. 378–380; Henry Scholberg (ed.), *op.cit*, pp. 86–87; James W. Laine, *Shivaji: Hindu King in Islamic India*, Oxford: Oxford University Press, 2003.

8 Guru Gobind Singh (born in 1666, Guru 1675–1708), the son of the ninth Guru, Guru Tegh Bahadur (born in 1621, Guru 1664–1675), was a scholar and military genius. In 1699 (the generally accepted date) he created the Khalsa order and the outward appearance of the Sikhs – the five Ks (five external signs of Sikh allegiance, required of Khalsa Sikhs) and the turban (in the case particularly of men) – is believed to date from this time. In 1708 he declared that there would be no more human Gurus after him, but that the Sikh Holy Scripture (Guru Granth Sahib) would become the eleventh and final Guru. See W. H. McLeod, *The Sikhs: History, Religion, and Society*, New York: Columbia University Press, 1989, pp. 44–46; W. Owen Cole, *Teach Yourself Sikhism*, London: Hodder & Stoughton, 1994, p. 75; W. Owen Cole, *Understanding Sikhism*, Edinburgh: Dunedin Academic Press, 2004, pp. 39–42; Eleanor Nesbitt, *Sikhism: A Very Short Introduction*, Oxford: Oxford University Press, 2nd edition, 2016, pp. 45–61; Nikky-Guninder Kaur Singh, *Sikhism: An Introduction*, London: I. B. Tauris, 2011, pp. 41–58; Pashaura Singh & Louis E. Fenech (eds), *The Oxford Handbook of Sikh Studies*, Oxford: Oxford University Press, 2014, pp. 22–25.

9 The Governor-General of India (1858–1947), commonly called Viceroy of India. He was originally the head of the British administration in India, and, later, after Pakistani and Indian independence in 1947, the Governor-General of the Union of India. The office was created in 1773, and was abolished in 1950. See Clive B. Mersey, *The Viceroys and Governors-General of India, 1757–1947*, London: T. and A. Constable Ltd, 1949.

10 Mohandas Karamchand Gandhi (1869–1948), the leader of the Indian independence movement against British rule. Born in a Hindu merchant caste family in Gujarat, western India, he trained in Law at the Inner Temple in London. His doctrine of civil disobedience and non-violent protest greatly influenced movements for civil rights and freedom across the world. See Clifford Manshardt (ed.), *The Mahatma and the Missionary: Selected Writings of Mohandas K. Gandhi*, Chicago: Henry Regnery Company, 1949; B.R. Nanda, *Mahatma Gandhi: A Biography*, Oxford: Oxford University Press, 1958; Ved Mehta, *Mahatma Gandhi and His Apostles*, New Haven & London: Yale University Press, 1977; Henry Scholberg (ed.), *op.cit.*, pp. 202–206; Judith Brown (ed.), *The Essential Works of Mahatma Gandhi*, Oxford: Oxford University Press, 2007; Mahatma Gandhi & Mahadev Desai, *An Autobiography: The Story of My Experiments with Truth*, Mumbai: Om Publications, 2009; Surjit Mansingh, *op.cit.*, pp. 145–150.

11 Rabindranath Tagore (1861–1941), a Bengali Brahmin, was a Bengali poet, playwright and author. He was one of the most outstanding and famous South Asians of

II The Life Story of Mr Ram Krishan (Prashar)

the twentieth century, especially contributing to Bengali literature and modern India. He was awarded the Nobel Prize for Literature in 1913. See Surjit Mansingh, *op.cit.*, pp. 401–403; Henry Scholberg (ed.), *op. cit.*, pp. 333–337.

12 Diwali is a mainly Hindu festival, although Sikhs and Jains also celebrate it for different reasons. Hindus celebrate the victory of Lord Rama over the evil demon-king Ravana. Diwali is called 'the festival of lights'. It is celebrated after Navaratri (meaning 'nine nights' in Sanskrit). It is a major festival dedicated to worshipping the Mother Goddess and celebrating the actions of the Lord Rama). See W. Owen Cole, p. 72, pp. 82–84; V. P. Hemant Kanitkar and Owen Cole, *Hinduism: An Introduction*, Abingdon: Bookpoint Ltd, 2010, pp. 97–102.

13 Shravan is the fifth month of the Hindu calendar (which begins with Chaitra – approximately April). The month of Shravan is considered highly auspicious for praying to Lord Shiva. A lot of Hindus observe fasts and perform pujas (Hindu worship involving offerings) during the month, especially on Monday. See http://hubpages.com/religion-philosophy/Shravan-Month-Somvar-Shukravar-Shanivar... [accessed: 13 May 2016].

14 Haripura is a village in the Surat district of Gujarat, India. During the Indian independence movement, it was the venue of the annual session of the Indian National Congress in February 1938, referred as the 'Haripura Session'. The most important resolution adopted was that pertaining to the Federal Scheme embodied in the Government of India Act of 1938. Sisir Kumar Bose & Sugata Bose (eds), *Subhas Chandra Bose: The Alternative Leadership*, Kolkata: Permanent Black, 2004; pp. 31, 59; Eric A. Vas, *Subhas Chandra Bose: The Man and His Times*, New Delhi: Lancer Publishers and Distributors, 2005, pp. 30–101.

15 Subhash [also spelled Subhas] Chandra Bose (1897–1945), one of the most prominent leaders of Indian freedom struggle, Congress President in 1938–1939 and founder of the Indian National Army (Azad Hind Fauj). He was elected President of the Haripura Session in 1938 (see no.14). See Henry Scholberg (ed.), *op. cit.*, pp. 182–185; See O. P. Ralhan, *Subhash Chandra Bose: His Struggle for Independence*, Delhi: Raj Publication, 1996; Marshall J. Getz, *Subhas Chandra Bose: A Biography*, Jefferson, North Carolina & London: McFarland, 2002; Sisir Kumar Bose and Sugata Bose (eds), *op.cit.*; Eric A. Vas, *op.cit.* As for Subhash Chandra Bose, there are a lot of aricles and books in Japanese.

16 Jawaharlal Nehru (1889–1964), the first Prime Minister of India. Born in Allahabad, in southern Uttar Pradesh in British India, he studied at Trinity College, Cambridge University, and trained to be a barrister at the Inner Temple in London. He was a disciple of Mahatma Gandhi, and was Prime Minister from 1947 until his death in 1964. Nehru is also considered to be the architect of the modern Indian state. See Stephen Ashton, *Jawaharlal Nehru*, Oxford: Oxford University Press, 1990; Henry Scholberg (ed.), *op.cit.*, pp. 219–222; Frank Moraes, *Jawaharlal Nehru: A Biography*, Mumbai: Jaico Publishing House, 2008.

17 Dr Rajendra Prasad (1884–1963), the first President of the Republic of India. He was a Kayastha (literate scribe caste) Hindu, and was born in Zeradai, in the Siwan district of Bihar. He was elected as the President of the Indian National Congress in

II The Life Story of Mr Ram Krishan (Prashar)

1934 and 1939. In 1950, after Indian independence, he became the first President. See Nirmal Kumar, *Rajendra Prasad and the Indian Freedom Struggle, 1917–1947*, Patriot Publishers, 1991; V. Grover, *Dr Rajendra Prasad*, New Delhi: Deep & Deep Publications, 1993.

18   Sardar Vallabhbhai Jhaverbhai Patel (1875–1950), born in Gujarat, one of Mohandas Gandhi's closest associates. He organized and led several *satyagraha* campaigns (nonviolent resistance developed by Mohandas Gandhi) during India's struggle for freedom from British rule. When India achieved independence in 1947, Patel became Home Minister and Deputy Prime Minister. He also presided over the most difficult task facing the nascent nation state, namely the integration of over 500 princely states into the Indian Union. He is known as the 'Iron Man of India'. See B. K. Ahluwalia, *Sardar Patel: A Life*, New Delhi: Sagar, 1974; Henry Scholberg (ed.), *op.cit.*, pp. 213–215.

19   Abul Kalam Muhiyuddin Ahmed Azad (1888–1958), commonly called Maulana Azad. An Indian scholar, a senior political leader of the Indian independence movement and the first Minister of Education after India's independence. See Ravindra Kumar, *Life and Works of Maulana Abul Kalam Azad*, Atlantic Publishers & Distributors, 1991; Surjit Mansingh, *op.cit.*, p. 50.

20   Durga Puja, an annual Hindu festival in South Asia. It celebrates worship of the Hindu Goddess Durga, marking the victory of Good over Evil (buffalo demon) Mahishasura. See Swami Satyananda Saraswati, *Durga Puja Beginner*, Devi Mandir, 2001, pp. 89–94; Banerjee Sudeshna, *Durga Puja: Yesterday, Today and Tomorrow*, New Delhi: Rupa & Co, 2004; Rachel Fell McDermott, *Revelry, Rivalry, and Longing for the Goddesses of Bengal: The Fortunes of Hindu Festivals*, New York: Columbia University Press, 2011.

21   Ramakrishna Paramahamsa (1836–1886), an Indian mystic and yogi during the nineteenth century. Later the Ramakrishna Mission was formed by his disciple Swami Vivekananda (1863–1902). It greatly influenced the spread of modern Hinduism. See Jeffrey J. Kripal, *Kali's Child: The Mystical and the Erotic in the Life and Teachings of Ramakirishna*, First Edition, Chicago: University of Chicago Press, 1995; Henry Scholberg (ed.), *op.cit.*, pp. 281–284; Amiya P. Sen, *Ramakrishna Paramahasa: Sadhaka of Dakshineswar*, London: Penguin Books Limited, 2010; Swami Tyagananda & Pravrajica Vrajaprana, *Interpreting Ramakrishna: Kali's Child Revisited*, Delhi: Motilal Banarsidass, 2010. For Swami Vivekananda, see Henry Scholberg (ed.), *op.cit.*, pp. 284–287.

22   Banda Bahadar (Bahadur), a follower of Guru Gobind Singh and leader of the Sikhs after Guru Gobind Singh's death in 1708. The declining Mughal Empire was faced with rebellion by many of its subjects, including the Sikhs. In 1710 Banda Singh (Banda Bahadar) led a revolt. See W. Owen Cole, *op.cit.*, p. 135; Pashaura Singh & Louis E. Fenech (eds), *op.cit.*, p. 52 and *passim*; Eleanor Nesbitt, *op.cit.*, pp. 58–59.

23   Guru Arjan (born in 1563, Guru 1581–1606), the fifth Guru of the Siks and the first Sikh martyr. He constructed the Ram Das Sarovar, the pool where bathers may remove all ills and impurities, and built the Harmandir Sahib (now Golden Temple), a physical focus for Sikh spirituality. He also collected the hymns that Sikh used in

II The Life Story of Mr Ram Krishan (Prashar)

their worship and put them together in one authoritative collection, the Adi Granth (the Sikh scripture), which he installed in the Harmandir Sahib in 1604. In 1606 he was killed by the Mughal authorities in Lahore. See W. Owen Cole (1994), *op.cit.*, pp. 73–74 and *passim*; W. Owen Cole (2004), *op.cit.*, pp. 33–35 and *passim*; Nikky-Guninder Kaur Singh, *op.cit.*, pp. 27–40; Eleanor Nesbitt, *op.cit.*, pp. 55–56 and *passim*.

24 Akali ('a follower of the timeless one') Movement, known as the Gurdwara (Sikh temple) Reform Movement or Gurdwara Agitation is how the Sikhs' long drawn campaign in the early 1920s for the liberation of their gurdwara is described. See Baldev Raj Nayar, *Minority Politics in the Punjab*, Princeton: Princeton University Press, 1966; Mohinder Singh, *The Akali Struggle: A Retrospect, Atlantic Publishers & Distributors*, 1988; Mohinder Singh, 'Akali Struggle: Past and Present' (pp. 191–210) and Ian J. Kerr, 'Fox and the Lions: The Akali Movement Revisited' (pp. 211–225), in Joseph T. O'Connell, Milton Israel & Willard G. Oxtoby (eds), *Sikh History and Religion in the Twentieth Century*, Toronto: University of Toronto, 1988; Teja Singh, *The Gurdwara Reform Movement and the Sikh Awakening*, Nabu Press, 2010.

25 Sukhmani Sahib is the name given to the set of hymns in 24 sections which appear in the Guru Granth Sahib, on page 262 of 1430. The Sukhmani literally means Treasure (Mani) of Peace (Sukh). This set of hymns (Bani) is very popular among the Sikhs. See Sukhmani Sahib Part 1-2: [http://www.rajkaregakhalsa.net/sukhmanisahib21.htm; http://www.rajkaregakhalsa.net/sukhmanisahib22.htm]. Japji Sahib, a Sikh prayer, appears at the beginning of Guru Granth Sahib. It is believed to be the first composition of Guru Nanak, and considered as the faith's most comprehensive essence. See H.S. Singha, *The Encyclopedia of Sikhism*, New Delhi: Hemkunt Press, 2009, p. 110.

26 Durgiana Mandir, a famous Hindu temple in Punjab (India) situated in the city of Amritsar. Although it derives its name from the Goddess Durga, its architecture is similar to the Sikhs' Harmandir Sahib in Amritsar. See S. Gajrani, *History, Religion and Culture of India*, Vol.1, Delhi: Isha Books, 2004, p. 220; Sunita Pant Bansal, *Encyclopaedia of India*, New Delhi: Smriti Books, 2005, p. 178.

27 Jallianwala Bagh, a public garden in Amritsar in the Punjab state of India. The garden houses a memorial of national importance, established in 1951 by the Government of India. It was to commemorate the massacre of peaceful celebrators, including unarmed women and children by British occupying forces, on the occasion of the Punjab New Year on 13 April 1919 in the Jallianwala Bagh Massacre. See G. Singh, *et al.* (eds), *Jallianwala Bagh Commemoration Volume and Amritsar and Our Duty to India*, Publication Bureau, Punjabi University, 1994. For the Jallianwala Bagh Massacre, see Alfred Draper, *The Amritsar Massacre: Twilight of the Raj (Echoes of War)*, London: Cassell, 1981; Dennis Judd, 'The Amritsar Massacre of 1919: Gandhi, the Raj and the Growth of Indian Nationalism, 1915–39', in Dennis Judd (ed.), *Empire: The British Imperial Experience from 1765 to the Present*, London: HarperCollins, 1996, pp. 258–272; Savita Narain, *The Historiography of the Jallianwala Bagh Massacre, 1919*, Surrey: Spantech and Lancer, 1998.

28 Colonel Reginald Edward Harry Dyer (1864–1927), a British Indian army officer responsible for the Jallianwala Bagh massacre in Amritsar in 1919. His nickname: 'The

Butcher of Amritsar'. He was born in Murree, in British India, now in Pakistan, and spent his childhood in Shimla. See T. R. Moreman, 'Dyer, Reginald Edward Harry (1864–1927)', *Oxford Dictionary of National Biography*, Oxford: Oxford University Press, 2004; Nigel Colett, *The Butcher of Amritsar: General Reginald Dyer*, London: Hambledon & London, 2005.

29 Lala Lajpat Rai (1865–1928), an Indian Punjabi writer and politician. He is chiefly remembered for his advocacy of a militant anti-British nationalism in the Indian National Congress and as a leader of the Hindu supremacy movement. He was an ardent worker for the Arya Samaj throughout his life (for Arya Samaj, see note no. 31). See Surjit Mansingh, *op.cit.*, p. 340; https://global.britannica.com/biography/Lala-Lajpat-Rai) [accessed: 2 September 2016].

30 Dr Saifuddin Kitchlew (1888–1963), an Indian freedom fighter, barrister and an Indian Muslim National leader. An Indian National Congress politician. See F. Z. Kichlew, *Freedom Fighter: The Story of Dr. Saifuddin Kitchlew*, Bognor Regis: New Horizon, 1979; Shyam Dua, *Luminous Life of Saifuddin Kitchlew*, Noida, India: Tiny Tots Publication, 2004

31 Arya Samaj, an Indian religious reform movement, promoting values and practices based on the infallibility of the Vedas. It also promoted Hindi and discouraged the use of Punjabi. The Arya Samaj was established in Bombay in 1885 by Dayanand Saraswati, author of *Satyarth Prakash*. There are now Arya Samaji mandirs in many countries. Arya Samaji [with 'i'] is the associated adjective, and denotes a member of the Arya Samaj. See John C. B. Webster (ed.), *Popular Religion in the Punjab Today*, Punjab: The Christian Institute of Sikh Studies, 1974, pp. 51–61; Kenneth W. Jones, *Arya Dharm: Hindu Consciousness in 19th-Century Punjab*, Berkeley: University of California Press, 1976; Satish Kumar Sharma, *Social Movements and Social Change: A Study of Arya Samaj and Untouchables in Punjab*, New Delhi: B. R. Publishing, 1985; Gulshan Swarup Saxena, *Arya Samaj Movement in India, 1875–1947*, Delhi: Commonwealth Publishers, 1990; Lala Lajpat Rai, The *Arya Samaj: An Account of Its Origin, Doctrines, and Activities: With a Biographical Sketch of the Founder*, Palala Press, 2015

32 The number of the Indian Army in volunteers was actually over 2.5 million men, including tank, artillery and airborn forces by the end of the Second World War. See Compton Mackenzie, *Eastern Epic*, London: Chatto & Windus, 1951; Daniel Marston, *The Indian Army and the End of the Raj*, Cambridge: Cambridge University Press, 2014, pp. 45–115.

33 Amrita Pritam (1919–2005), an Indian writer and poet, writing in Punjabi and Hindi. The first prominent woman Punjabi poet, novelist and essayist. She is equally well known on both sides of India-Pakistan border. One of her most important poems is *Ajj Waris Shah Nu (Today I Invoke Waris Shah)*. See Darshan Singh Maini, *Studies in Punjabi Poetry*, Vikas Publishing, 1979; Uma Trilok, *Amrita Imroz: A Love Story*, New Delhi: Penguin India, 2006.

34 Waris Shah, a Punjabi Sufi poet, author of the most celebrated Punjabi romance *Hir Ranjha*, based on the traditional folk tale of Hir and her lover Ranjha. He is also called the 'Shakespeare of Punjabi language'. *Hir Ranjha*, is one of several popular

II   The Life Story of Mr Ram Krishan (Prashar)

tragic romances of Punjab. Although there are several poetic narrations of the story, the most famous one is written by Waris Shah in 1766. See Henry Scholberg (ed.), *op.cit.*, pp. 313–315; R.M. Chopra, *Great Sufi Poets of the Punjab*, Calcutta: Iran Society, 1999.

35 Krishan Chander (1914–1977), an Urdu/Hindi writer of short stories and novels and a screenwriter for Bollywood. While one of his famous novels is *Ek Gadhe Ki Sarguzasht (Autobiography of a Donkey)*, his famous short stories include *Annadata (The Giver of Grain)* and *Ham Valshi Hain (We are Savages)*. See *Daily Times* (3 February 2014). See https://en.wikipedia.org/wiki/Krishan_Chander [accessed: 2 September 2016].

36 Saadat Hasan Manto (1912–1955), an Indo-Pakistani writer and playwright. He chronicled the chaos that prevailed, during and after the Partition of India in 1947. *Toba Tek Singh* is his short story published in 1955. It follows inmates in a Lahore asylum, some of whom are to be transferred to India following the independence of Pakistan in 1947. See Saadat Hasan Manto on Penguin Books India; http://www.penguinbooksindia.com/en/content/saadat-hasan-manto; Toba Tek Singh – About the story – Columbia University: http://www.columbia.edu/itc/mealac/pritchett/00urdu/tobateksingh/storynotes.html [accessed: 5 September 2016]; Toba Tek Singh by Saadat Hasan Manto: http://www.sacw.ne/partition/tobateksingh.html; *Manto Naama: The Life of Saadat Hasan Manto*, English translation of the above by Jai Ratan, Roli Books, 1998; Stephen Alter, 'Madness and Partition: The Short Stories of Saadat Hasan Manto', Alif: *Journal of Comparative Poetics*, No.14, 1994.

37 Nankana Sahib, a city and capital of Nankana Sahib District in the Punjab province of Pakistan. It is named after the first Guru of the Sikhs, Guru Nanak (1469–1539) as he was born here and first began preaching here. It is now an important and popular pilgrimage site for Sikhs from all over the world. See Historical Gurdwaras: NANKANA SAHIB old.sgpc.net/historical-gurdwaras/gurdwaras_in_pakistan.asp [accessed: 2 September 2016]; Nankana becomes a district: http://www.dawn.com/2005/05/10/nat43.htm [accessed: 2 September 2016].

38 Alan Campbell-Johnson, *Mission with Mountbatten: Foreword by the Earl Mountbatten of Burma*, Macmillan Publishing Co., 1985, pp. 280–281.

39 Sarojini Naidu (1879–1949), an Indian independence activist, politician and poet. She was the second Indian woman to become the President of the Indian National Congress. She is known as 'the Nightingale of India'. Being one of the most famous heroines of the twentieth century, her birthday is celebrated as 'Women's Day'. See Padmini Sengupta, *Sarojini Naidu*, New Delhi: Sahitya Akademi, 1997; Henry Scholberg (ed.), *op.cit.*, pp. 330–333.

40 Alan Campbell-Johnson, *op.cit.*, p. 284.

41 Harivansh Rai Bachchan (1907–2003), one of the most acclaimed Hindi-language poets of the twentieth century. His books include his long poem *Madhushala (The House of Wine)*. His son is the megastar, Amitabh Bachchan. See http://global.britannica.com/biography/Harivansh-Rai-Bachchan; http://www.amazon.in/Books-Harivansh-Rai-Bachchan/s?ie=UTF8&page=1&rh=n%... [accessed: 2 Septem-

ber 2016].

42 Pandit Banarsidas Chaturvedi (1892–1985), a Hindi-language writer and journalist. He wrote extensively about the predicament of Indians (mainly indentured labourers [Girmitiya]) in Fiji. The system of the labourers there was formally ended in 1920. See A. Datta, *Encyclopaedia of Indian Literature: A-Devo*, New Delhi: Sahitya Akademi, 1987.

43 Alfred Herbert Limited, was Britain's largest machine tool manufacturing business and also, at one time, one of the world's largest machine tool companies. The business was founded in 1888 (Roderick C. Floud, *The British Machine Tool Industry, 1850–1914*, Cambridge: Cambridge University Press, 1976; Roger Lloyd-Jones & Myrddin John Lewis, *Alfred Herbert Ltd and the British Machine Tool Industry, 1887–1983*, Aldershot: Ashgate, 2006.

44 For the end of butter rationing in 1954, see http://news.bbc.co.uk/onthisday/hi/dates/stories/july/4/newsid_3818000/3818563.stm [accessed: 8 September 2016].

45 For the destruction of Coventry, David McGrory, *Coventry at War*, Stroud: The History Press, 1997; David McGrory, *Coventry's Blitz*, Stroud: Amberley, 2015.

46 Sindhis are an ethnic group, originating from Sindh, a province of Pakistan. After the 1947 partition of India and Pakistan, many Sindhi Hindus migrated to India and some later to other parts of the world. The religious belief and practice of Sindhis comprises elements of both Hindu and Sikh traditions. For the history of Sindhis, see Claude Markovits, *The Global World of Indian Merchants, 1750–1947*, Cambridge: Cambridge University Press, 2000; Matthew A. Cook & Michael Boivin (eds), *Interpreting the Sindhi World: Essays on Society and History*, Oxford: Oxford University Press, 2010; Nandita Bhavnani, *The Making of Exile: Sindhi Hindus and the Partition of India*, Chennai: Tranquebar, 2014.

47 For the Race Relations Acts (in 1965, 1968 and 1976), see Christina Julios, *Contemporary British Identity: English Language, Migrants and Public Discourse*, Aldershot: Ashgate, 2008, pp. 97–100.

48 Enoch Powell, MBE (1912–1998), a British politician, classical scholar, poet, writer, and soldier. He served as a Conservative MP (1950–1974) and Minister of Sir Edward Heath (1960–1963). His controversial 'Rivers of Blood' speech in Birmingham in 1968 is very famous. After then he was expelled from the Conservative Party and later stood as a Unionist MP from Northern Ireland. For Powell, see Rex Collings (selected), *Reflections of a Statesman: The Writings and Speeches of Enoch Powell*, London: Bellew Publishing, 1991; Simon Heffer, *Like the Roman: the Life of Enoch Powell*, London: Faber and Faber, 2008; Lord Howard of Rising (ed.), *Enoch at 100: A Re-evaluation of the Life, Politics and Philosophy of Enoch Powell*, London: Biteback Publishing, 2012.

49 The first Indian Workers' Association was founded in London in the 1930s, while another was set up in Coventry in 1938. Immigrant workers from India focused on agitating for Indian independence. In 1958 the Indian Workers' Association (GB) was set up to provide a central national body to co-ordinate the activities of the local groups. It aimed to improve conditions for immigrant workers, working alongside the mainstream British labour movement. Most of them were Sikhs. See DeWitt

John, *Indian Workers' Associations in Britain*, Oxford: Oxford University Press, 1969; Sasha Josephides, *Towards a History of Indian Workers' Associations*, Coventry: Centre for Research in Ethnic Relations, University of Warwick, 1991; John King, *Three Asian Associations in Britain*, Coventry: Centre for Research in Ethnic Relations, University of Warwick, 1994; Talvinder Gill, 'The Indian Workers' Association Coventry 1938–1990: Political and Social Action', *South Asian History and Culture*, Vol.4, Issue 4, 2013.

50 For social activities of Asians including the Indian Cultural and Welfare Society, see Pippa Virdee, *Coming to Coventry: Stories from the South Asian Pioneers*, Coventry: The Herbert, 2006, pp. 93–105.

51 For Vyjayanthimala's visit to Coventry, see *Ibid*., pp. 94–97.

52 Swami Satyamitranandji (1932–), a Hindu spiritual guru, is usually known as Swami Satyamitranand Giri Ji. He is the founder of Bharat Mata Mandir, a famous temple in Haridwar, which was inaugurated by the then Indian Prime Minister Indira Gandhi in 1983. See Bharatmatamandir (http://www.bharatmatamandir.co.in/?page_id=264) [accessed: 2 September 2016].

53 Morari Bapu, real name Moraridas Prabhudas Hariyani (1946–), a popular Hindu *kathakar* (bard), born in Gujarat. He has given nine day-long sermons (*katha*s) in both Gujarati and Hindi in many parts of the world. See http://www.moraribapu.org/new_2013/) [accessed: 2 September 2016]; Ram Katha by Morari Bapu (Audio and Video) [1]; http://www.moraribapu.org/ramkatha_katha_audio&videos.htmal.

54 A group commonly known as 'Hare Krishnas' or 'Hare Krishna movement' is 'International Society for Krishna Consciousness' (ISKCON). The organisation was founded in 1966 in New York City by A.C.Bhaktivedanta Swami Prabhupada who is worshipped by followers as Guru and spiritual master. The core beliefs are based on select traditional Hindu scriptures. The ISKCON devotees worship Krishna as the highest form of God. A sixteen-word Hare Krishna mantra or the Maha Mantra contains the names of God Krishna and Rama.

The mantra:
Hare Krishna Hare Krishna
Krishna Krishna Hare Hare
Hare Rama Hare Rama
Rama Rama Hare Hare

See Kim Knott, *My Sweet Lord: Hare Krishna Movement*, Wellingborough: The Aquarian Press, 1986; Edwin F. Bryant & Maria Ekstrand (eds), *The Hare Krishna Movement: The Postcharismatic Fate of a Religious Transplant*, New York: Columbia University Press, 2004; Graham Cole Dwyer & Richard J. Cole (eds), *The Hare Krishna Movement: Forty Years of Chant and Change*, London: I. B. Tauris, 2007.

55 A *murti* is a statue of a god or goddess and in English Hindu devotees often use the word 'deity' for a *murti*. In Jaipur, Rajasthan, craftsmen continue the tradition of carving marble *murti*s.

56 Nagar Kirtan – procession headed by the Guru Granth Sahib in a vehicle escorted by Panj Piare, five Sikhs in traditional dress. This takes place on a Sunday following the festival of Vaisakhi. Vaisakhi, New Year's Day, the first day of the month of

II The Life Story of Mr Ram Krishan (Prashar)

Vaisakh, is celebrated on or near 13 April. (In the particular Nanakshahi calendar which Sikh authorities in Amritsar approved in the twenty-first century Vaisakhi is on April 14.) It marks the day in 1699 when Guru Gobind Singh formed the Khalsa, the Sikh brotherhood. See W. Owen Cole (1994), *op.cit.*, pp. 81–83; W. Owen Cole (2004), *op.cit.*, pp. 120–121; Nikky-Guninder Kaur Singh, *op.cit.*, p. 235 and *passim*.)

57 Ravan Dahan (burning of Ravana) is celebrated after dark on Dassehra, i.e. about 18 days before Diwali. In the Ramayana epic Ravana is the demon king of Lanka who abducts Sita, Lord Rama's wife. Lord Rama's victory over the ten-headed demon king Ravana is celebrated – as a victory of good over evil – by settting fire to a gigantic effigy of Ravana, stuffed with fireworks, i.e. the victory of Good over Evil.

58 The Sikh community was still in second place with 4.64 per cent of the local population at the time of the 2001 census but by 2011 Muslims had increased from 3.88 per cent to 7.47 per cent whereas Sikhs had only increased to 5.02 per cent. See Appendix 6, pp. 132–133.

59 Hindus constituted 2.58 per cent of Coventry's population in 2001 and 3.52 per cent in 2011. See Appendix 6, pp. 132–133.

60 The British National Party (BNP) is a British far-right political party formed as a splinter group from the National Front (NF) by John Tyndall in 1982. It restricted membership to 'indigenous British' people until 2010, when there was a legal challenge to its constitution. Nick Griffin is a former national organiser of the National Front, led the BNP from 2009 to 2014. The NF, a British far right, racial nationalist, neo-fascist, whites-only political party, was formed in 1966. The party split in 1982, when the breakaway BNP was formed. For the BNP, see Nigel Copsey & Graham Macklin (eds), *The British National Party: Contemporary Perspectives*, London: Routledge, 2011; Matthew J. Goodwin, *New British Fascism: Rise of the British National Party*, London: Routledge, 2011. For the NF, see Richard Thurlow, *Fascism in Britain: From Oswald Mosley's Blackshirts to the National Front*, London: I. B. Tauris Publishers, 1988; Julie V. Gottlieb & Thomas P. Linehan (eds), *The Culture of Fascism: Visions of the Far Right in Britain*, London: I. B. Tauris, 2004.

III
Eleanor's contribution to Ram's story

III Eleanor's contribution to Ram's story

Professor Sato has asked me, as Ram Krishan's wife, to add a few words about our life stories in relation to each other. Sometimes I sum this up by saying that I was the daughter of a Christian priest and then married a Hindu priest. By this I mean that my father became a priest in the Church of England and Ram was born into a Brahmin family and knows how to conduct Hindu rites. Religious activity and commitment have been a strong feature of my family's life and have given me plenty to compare. They have connected with my professional work in the academic fields of religious studies and religious education.

I was born in 1951 in Bournemouth (on the south coast of England) and I attended primary and secondary school there, although my childhood home was the other side of the river Stour in the much older town of Christchurch. My father, William Ralph Nesbitt, grew up in Yorkshire and worked in Bournemouth's telephone exchange. He devoted his spare time to a local church as a lay reader and he also visited outlying churches to conduct services. He later completed his theological training and was ordained in Winchester cathedral, as a non-stipendiary priest, while I was an undergraduate.

My parents and I on holiday in Folkstone in c. 1957.

My mother, Martha Eleanor née Lidbetter, was known as Pattie. She was originally from London and had then lived in Hertfordshire. She took pride in being the best of housewives – expertly cooking, cleaning, gardening and making and repairing clothes. She was a skilled embroidress and loved playing the piano. She had met my father on a rare holiday, a summer school for Sunday School teachers, and they maintained their courtship by post for years until, during World War II, my father came to Southampton (despite its being a prime military target) in order to be nearer to her. They married in 1944.

82 Hurn Way, Christchurch, my childhood home.

My childhood was happy. I loved our extensive garden and my succession of pets, especially my white cat,

III Eleanor's contribution to Ram's story

Persil. Homework took up increasing amounts of time but I managed to read extensively, to write poems and to paint flowering plants, usually for greeting cards. Life followed a clear weekly pattern and each year we had a two-week holiday. Aged just ten I went abroad with my parents for the first time. We stayed in northern France and I was excited by the opportunity to start learning another language.

I made many friends at my secondary school, Talbot Heath, I did well in academic subjects and opted for French, Latin and Greek at A level. My goal from the age of eight was to study at Cambridge – my parents and I had stayed there that summer and I had fallen in love with the river, the ducks and willow trees. At 17, I duly won scholarships to colleges in the universities of both Oxford and Cambridge to study classics i.e. Latin, Greek, ancient history, philosophy and literature. In 1969 I packed my new wooden trunk and went up to Girton College, Cambridge for four years: after two years of classics I proceeded to two years of the Theological and Religious Studies Tripos. By some premonition, perhaps, I had in fact entered Girton to study 'Oriental Studies', but I did not follow this up as I had at that time no idea which language or region I wished to study.

At Cambridge I sampled some of the many religious organisations and congregations on offer. In 1971 I commenced the study of Theology. That same summer, with a friend, Gill Westcott, I attended my first Quaker meeting. The lack of dogma and liturgy plus the tranquillity of people's faces as they sat in silence drew me in. In about 1980 I became a Member of the Religious Society of Friends (Quakers).

I attended a lecture by a south Indian theologian, Paul Sudhakar, and from that time my answer to people's question, 'What will you do after graduating?' was 'I will go to India'. (I don't recall a moment of doubt about this, even though I was usually tormented by indecision about even the tiniest steps.) With that in mind I decided that the most practicable way to equip myself to live usefully in India was to train to be a teacher, as there were English-medium schools there. In 1973 I began my Post-Graduate Certificate in Education course – specialising in religious education and French – at Oxford. A few months earlier I had pursued a summer course at St George's College, Jerusalem, where I met Mary Rogers (a former Girton classicist) who had spent many years in India. She gave me the addresses of two headmistresses. I wrote to both, offering my services. Miss Ruth Compton, the headmistress of All Saints' School, Naini Tal, Uttar Pradesh offered me a job as teacher of English.

When I asked her what I might read in preparation for my appointment she suggested Jim Corbett's *Man-Eaters of Kumaon*.[1] So I arrived in the Himalayan foothills in September 1974, knowing only that this had been the haunt of man-eating tigers. All Saints' School had been set up by the Diocese of Lucknow, for the education of 'poor Anglo-Indian girls' and had been threatened by closure in 1947, after the exodus of Anglo-Indian families following India's Partition. The poet, Sarojini Naidu,[2] the then state governor, had intervened to save the school.

III Eleanor's contribution to Ram's story

By 1974 most pupils were the daughters of Punjabi families who had fled across the new border and been compensated for their farmland with uncultivated land near the foothills. Through hard work, the jungle had become flourishing fields of wheat and sugarcane and families could therefore give their daughters a 'convent education', so increasing their eligibility to marry a suitable husband. About half my students were Hindu and about half were Sikhs. A minority were from other backgrounds – the (Christian) teachers' children plus some (Buddhist) Tibetan refugees and one or two Muslims and a Zoroastrian. In Naini Tal, as an escort to Sikh pupils on Guru Nanak's birthday, I visited the lake-side gurdwara. I had only once before visited a gurdwara – the Sis Ganj gurdwara in Delhi, during my first week in India.

I lived in the school, and made friends with colleagues and in the town. Work was demanding, but life in those mountains was magical. The profusion of wild flowers amazed me. I drew and painted plants whenever time allowed, and friends in the local degree college's botany department identified them all for me. My period in India coincided with the Emergency, a regime imposed by the Prime Minister, Mrs Indira Gandhi. This included a harsh programme of enforced family planning and stringent inspection of public transport in Delhi. Worthy slogans were stencilled on the buses – a valuable aid to my study of Hindi.

For three winter months the school closed because of the intense cold, leaving me free to roam India. During term-time I seized opportunities to explore the hills. My vacation travels included the journey across north India, via Kanpur and Banaras, to my Cambridge friend Stephen Barton's wedding near the border with Bangladesh; travel around Rajasthan's palaces and temples; a brief stint with Delhi University students doing 'social work' among tribal people in the Chambal Valley (then noted for the exploits and surrender of dangerous dacoits); a memorable stay in Maharashtra, visiting cave temples, and a journey south through Bombay and Goa to the wonders of Kerala and Tamil Nadu. My companions on this expedition were my All Saints' colleague, Kamla Sawhney, and my Girton friend, Gill Westcott. From 1975 to 1977 I was hosted by members of Kamla's family in many parts of India, and especially by her brother in New Delhi and her sister in Chandigarh. Importantly, too, Kamla and Mataji (her mother) had decided that they would encourage me in learning Hindi rather than their mother-tongue, Punjabi, as Hindi was more widely spoken.

In February 1977 my father ventured to India and I introduced him to beloved people and places before re-

My father and I at the Taj Mahal, Agra in 1977.

III Eleanor's contribution to Ram's story

turning to the UK with him. I wanted to build on my experience in India by teaching in one of the British cities where many people from India, Pakistan and Bangladesh were now living. A number of local education authorities were setting up initiatives for teaching 'English as a second language'. I was called for interview to Coventry and joined the newly established Minority Group Support Service there. Most of my students in school were Punjabi Sikhs and so too were the adults whom I taught in evening classes.

Alongside teaching I kept notes of my discoveries about religious and cultural details of my students' lives. Increasingly I realised that my next step would be post-graduate study of Sikhism. My exploratory letter to the University of Nottingham coincided with the Revd Dr Douglas Davies, in the Theology faculty, having re-advertised a funded research post for study of the local Sikh community. This enabled me to investigate the ways in which Sikhs' traditions were continuing and adapting in Nottingham. I quickly realised that there were three local Sikh communities and that each community had a separate gurdwara and had stereotypical perceptions of the other communities.

After my year in Nottingham I returned to Coventry where I combined working as a supply teacher in Coventry schools with academic assignments – writing entries for the *Oxford Dictionary of World Religions* (thanks to Professor John Bowker) and (thanks to Professor Robert Jackson), when the need arose, teaching undergraduate teacher trainees at the University of Warwick about the Hindu tradition. In the summer of 1984 I carried out some funded research for the university, a study of young British Hindus' 'formal religious nurture' i.e. the supplementary classes which some attended in religion and in Hindi or Gujarati language. Also in 1984 I was one of the co-founders of the still flourishing, interdisciplinary Punjab Research Group. From 1986 I was to work with Bob Jackson on a succession of research projects on the religious socialisation of young Christians, Hindus and Sikhs and, in 1994, I was a founder editor of the (now) *Journal of Punjab Studies*.

Ram and I first met in 1986 (I think) when I visited his temple to check out some information for a religious education teacher who had consulted me about the Hindu items that he had assembled to resource religious education in Warwickshire. Ram and I next met on the number 2 bus in Coventry and, after that, he coached me in the Hindi language for two examinations. We married in 1990. As I look back over the past 27 years, other people's questions and comments shed some light on what has brought and kept us together.

My father, the Revd Ralph Nesbitt, and I in our garden after the wedding in 1990.

One visitor from New Delhi, who has known me

III Eleanor's contribution to Ram's story

from the mid-1970s, long before our marriage, remarked that our relationship made sense to her because she realised that Ram and I had shared interests, especially an enthusiasm for literature. On another occasion, my response to a family member's dismissal of Ram's knowledge of Sanskrit as being a totally useless skill was that actually Ram's ease in reciting Sanskrit was one thing that had particularly impressed me. As a classicist I admired anyone with such a ready command of an ancient language.

What is more, Ram and I are both involved in interfaith activity, which is coupled with keen involvement in our own faith community. In my case this is the local Quaker Meeting and the Religious Society of Friends (Quakers) nationally. In Ram's case it is the Hindu temple and the UK Hindu community more generally. He is a trustee of the Coventry Multi-Faith Forum while I have devoted a lot of my time to the study of different religious groups and to sharing my ideas of 'interfaith pilgrimage'. In fact, a book that I wrote, *Interfaith Pilgrims: Living Truths and Truthful Living*, notes the contribution of Hindu ideas and ways of worship to my approach to life. What particularly interests me is how individuals' insights are deepened, challenged and informed by engaging with others in our diverse society.

My professional work has benefited from Ram's experience as a Hindu and from his gift for finding material relevant to my various projects, starting with my study of the lives of Hindu children. He has always been ready to answer the questions of other writers, too, on Hindu subjects, so his name appears in various acknowledgements. At the same time, he is a frequent attender at Coventry Quaker Meeting as well as participating in other Quaker events – often ones at which I am a speaker. I help him to host the groups of schoolchildren who visit the temple as part of their religious education curriculum and other enquirers who want to find out more about Hinduism. Hindus generously commend me for being vegetarian and for making an effort to speak Hindi.

Ram is supportive of my activities as an aspiring poet (in English). He is a champion of Hindi, Urdu and Punjabi poetry: one of my sorrows is that I can't relish poetry in these languages fully, as I need quite a bit of explanation to help me to understand them. However, I enjoy hearing about *mushaira*s and *kavi sammelan*s (gatherings of poets) and knowing that Ram is in touch with a number of Hindi writers.

We both love traveling to new places as well as revisiting places that hold happy memories for us. I was able to introduce him to pilgrimage sites in South India and the beautiful countryside, backwaters and coast of Kerala. He managed to convince me that cruises were an excellent means of seeing the world and meeting people, including especially the attentive crew members from (usually) various Asian countries.

His sociability, his readiness to make new friends and his recall of conversations, often with fleeting acquaintances, are definite pluses. So, too, is his unfailing enthusiasm for debate, especially about politics.

III Eleanor's contribution to Ram's story

Our respective families have enriched our lives in both the UK and India: Ram's family in Coventry, Birmingham, Cambridgeshire and elsewhere and mine in Dorset, Yorkshire and (now) Berkshire, where my cousin Rosy Droar has settled. Ever since my period teaching in Naini Tal, I have been part of another Punjabi family, the family of Kamla Sawhney, my colleague at All Saints' School. So, not only have I stayed with Ram's brother Hari's extended family in Nawanshahr but Ram has been welcomed to the homes of Kamla's relatives in different parts of North India. I remember Kamla's mother, my Mataji, asking anxiously how I had been received by my inlaws on my first visit to their house. It was good to hear later that, on that first visit to Nawanshahr, my brother-in-law, Hari, called Ram to say how lucky he was to have me as his wife.

Friends often ask me whether I make frequent visits to India. Generally I explain that, with the television set on South Asian channels every day and conversation all around me in Punjabi and Hindi, I feel less need to visit India in a geographical sense.

Ram has always been supportive of my career. Since marrying him I have progressed from a senior research fellowship to being professor in religions and education. I was principal investigator for three externally funded research projects. My final research project was a study of young people's religious identity formation in 'mixed-faith' families. In retirement I continue to write – poetry as well as for academic publications.

Without a shadow of a doubt my life has been enriched by marriage to Ram and the support of his family and wider Hindu community. Punjab has been a strong element in my life, thanks to Kamla's introduction, followed by my immersion in Sikh studies, and – thanks to Ram – I get plenty of practical experience, making *muliwale paranthe* (flatbreads stuffed with grated and spiced white radish) and attempting to master Punjabi dishes.

Ram and I with our granddaughter Manisha in Coventry in about 2002.

Our life together is an unfailingly interesting enterprise, involving plenty of surprises and plenty of humour.

Eleanor Nesbitt
20 August 2015

III Eleanor's contribution to Ram's story

Notes

1. James Edward Jim Corbett (1875–1955), a British-Indian hunter and tracker-turned-conservationist, naturalist and writer. He is famous for hunting a large number of man-eating tigers and leopards in India. After 1947, he retired to Nyeri, Kenya. After his retirement he wrote *Man-Eaters of Kumaon, Jungle Lore*, and other books recounting his hunts and experiences. He was born of Irish ancestry in the town of Nainital in the Kumaon region of the Himalayas (now in the Indian state of Uttarakhand). See Durga Charan Kala, *Jim Corbett of Kumaon*, Delhi: Ravi Dayal Publishers, 1979; Jerry A. Jaleel, *Under the Shadow of Man-eaters: The Life and Legend of Jim Corbett of Kumaon*, London: Orient Longman, 2001; Reeta Dutta Gupta, *Jim Corbett: The Hunter Conservationist*, New Delhi: Rup & Company, 2006.
2. For Sarojini Naidu (1879–1949), see note no. 39 of the Life Story of Mr Ram Krishan, p. 66.

IV
Appendices

IV   Appendices

Appendix 1: Photo memories of Mr Ram Krishan and his family

Nawanshahr, 1964 or 1965. Left to right: my mother, Rattan Devi, my sister-in-law, Indira, Hari Krishan's wife, my father, Pandit Malawa Ram (back), my niece, Satyabhama's eldest daughter, Meenakshi, and her doll, my brother, Hari Krishan Bhakta and my sister, Satyabhama.

An early photo of me in England.

Here I am in bed in King Edward VII Memorial Chest Hospital, Hertford Hill, Hatton, Warwickshire. I spent about six months here being treated for tuberculosis. I have very happy memories of the National Health Service (in probably 1956–1957).

IV   Appendices

My mother, Rattan Devi, feeding my younger brother, Hari Krishan, during his engagement (*kurmai*) ceremony in Nawanshahr in 1966.

Outside my family's house in Nawanshahr. My father, Pandit Malawa Ram, is sitting in the centre of the front row with friends and relatives.

Rajni and Rajeev as small children in about 1967.

Rajni, aged 2, in the garden of 23 Dugdale Road, Coventry.

Rajni, Rajeev and Rita in about 1976.

IV   Appendices

Rita as a child.

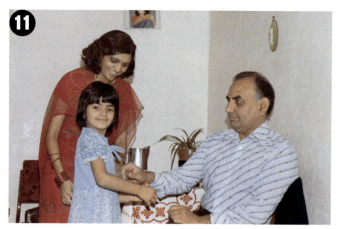

Me with my first wife, Adesh Kanta, and our children, Rajeev, Rajni and Rita.

Rita tying a *rakhi* (thread) on my right wrist on Raksha Bandhan day.

Rajni giving me a sweet.   Rajni with her cousins.

IV   Appendices

My father-in-law and mother-in-law watch as I garland Eleanor outside Coventry Register Office in 1990.

Eleanor signing the marriage register in Coventry Register Office in July 1990.

Outside Coventry Register Office (Cheylesmore Manor House) with family and friends.

Outside Coventry Register Office with family and friends.

IV   Appendices

Eleanor with her father, the Revd Ralph Nesbitt, in our garden after the wedding, in 1990.

My second wife, Eleanor, and I cutting our wedding cake, in our house in Coventry.

Eleanor, Rajni and I performing *arati* (an act of worship) at the *chaunki* (a thanksgiving event) in the Hindu Temple, Coventry soon after our marriage, in 1990.

Eleanor and I with friends in the Quaker Meeting House, Coventry, in 1990 at a party to celebrate our marriage. From left to right: Sheetal Anand, Eleanor Jackson, Rita Anand, Robert Jackson, me, Eleanor, Subhash Anand (General Secretary, Hindu Temple Society), Ahmed Lakdawala.

IV   Appendices

We have enjoyed hosting many visitors in our home. The first was Ella, a Quaker from Alaska in August 1990.

My elder daughter, Rajni, and I in Devon in the early 1990s.

Rajni, her fiancé Bernard, Eleanor and I at Land's End, Cornwall in 1995.

Rajni and I with Eleanor, on the day she received her doctorate at the University of Warwick in 1995.

Rajni with me on her wedding day, July 1996.

IV Appendices

20 July 1996, in the garden. Left to right: Rita, Eleanor, Rajni, me and Rajeev.

Rajieev, Rajni and Rita.

My step-mother-in-law, Kathleen, with Rajni and me – and Meggie, Kathleen's dog, in Kathleen's garden c. 1994.

My step-mother-in-law, Kathleen, celebrating her 80th birthday in 1996 with Michael and Barbara, my step-brother- and sister-in-law, who have always made me so welcome.

IV   Appendices

Me with my granddaughter, Manisha.

Same as fig. 31.

Bernard and Rajni with their daughter, Manisha.

My son-in-law Bernard with Rajni and their daughter Manisha at Hatton, Warwickshire.

IV   Appendices

In October 2006 this picture of my granddaughter Manisha appeared in the local papers, and we woke up to see a huge poster of her just opposite our window outside the school across the road.

Rajni, Bernard and Manisha at a friend's daughter's marriage in 2014.

My son, Rajeev, and I in Majorca on holiday.

Me with Rajeev's daughter, Rachna.

IV Appendices

Me with my younger daughter, Rita, in Coventry.

Me with my younger daughter, Rita, son-in-law, Alex, and their elder son, Sam in 2007.

Me with my grandsons, Sam (left) and Ben (right).

My grandsons, Sam and Ben, in Coventry in 2011.

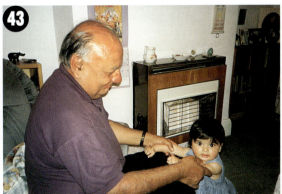
Me with my granddaughter, Rachna about 1996/7.

IV Appendices

Me with my sister, Satyabhama, in England.

My eldest niece, Meenakshi (Satyabhama's daughter), with her husband, Ashok at a party in Cambridgeshire, UK.

My niece Seema with Anh and family at their wedding.

Our family is truly multicultural: photos from the wedding of my sister's middle daughter, Seema, to Anh in London in 2000.

IV   Appendices

Me in the oldest part of the family house in Nawanshahr in 1993.

My eldest nephew, Navneet, in my brother's family pharmacy in Nawanshahr, Punjab in 1993.

My middle nephew, Ramneek, welcomes me to the family pharmacy, Nawanshahr, in 1993, with my brother Hari Krishan.

My youngest nephew, Puneet, in 1993. He took Eleanor and me from Nawanshahr to visit Hindu pilgrimage places in the hills.

My brother Hari Krishan and sister-in-law Indira in Nawanshahr in 1993.

My eldest nephew, Navneet, and I in June 2004 in London.

IV   Appendices

My son Rajeev and my eldest nephew, Navneet, in our house in Coventry during his visit to England in June 2004.

My younger brother, Hari Krishan, and my sister-in-law, Indira, outside the family home in Nawanshahr in 2006.

At the Golden Temple, Amritsar, with my brother's family in 2006. From left to right (back row) Neetu, Ram Krishan, Neeru, Eleanor, Indira. (front row) Isha, Rohan, Pankaj and Neeraj.

IV   Appendices

Hari and Indira at a family wedding in Punjab in 2006.

My brother's daughters-in-law, Neetu and Neeru, in Nawanshahr in 2006.

Me with my brother's granddaughter, Isha, in Nawanshahr in 2006.

My brother's grandchildren, Rohan, Pankaj, Isha and Neeraj, in Nawanshahr in 2006.

IV   Appendices

Ruins of St Michael's church, the 'old cathedral', Coventry, 2015

Me standing at the east end of the cathedral ruins, by the 'Litany of Reconciliation' and two poppy wreaths, 2015.

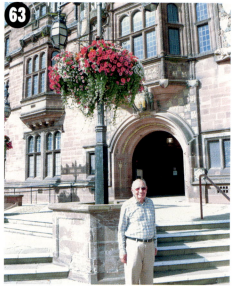

In front of the Council House, Coventry, 2015.

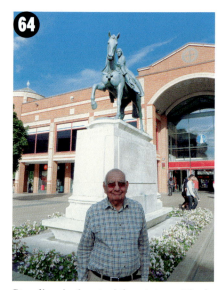

Standing in front of the statue of Lady Godiva in Broadgate, Coventry, 2015.

Me standing in St Patrick's Road, where I used to live, 2015.

My former home in St Patrick's Road, 2015.

IV   Appendices

Appendix 2: The Indian Cultural and Welfare Society (ICWS)

Office bearers of the Indian Cultural and Welfare Society (ICWS) of which I was a founding member: Pritam Das Khosla, Raj Kumar Sharda, Kedarnath Kalia and myself (bottom right). The ICWS invited Bollywood film directors, actors and actresses and also showed films in the Savoy Cinema (now a bingo hall), Radford, Coventry.

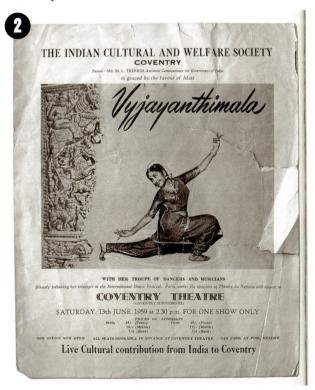

Indian Cultural and Welfare Society poster, 1959, for Vyjayanthimala's performance at Coventry Theatre (now demolished). People came from Nottingham, Leicester and further afield. (Janak Raj Chibba and I) [Virdee 1996, p. 96].

IV   Appendices

Bollywood film actress, Vyjayanthimala, in Coventry in 1959 in the Coventry Theatre with members of the ICWS. (I am wearing a white jacket.)

Vyjayanthimala at a reception in the Savoy cinema, Coventry.

IV   Appendices

Myself and other members of the ICWS when Vyjayanthimala visited the Scala Theatre, London in 1959.

Sohrab Modi (1897–1984) (centre) was a well-known film actor and director. His film *Jhansi ki Rani* won awards. He came to Coventry at the invitation of the ICWS. Jaganath Kalia is on the left and I am on the right (in dark suit).

This photo shows me, Kedarnath Kalia and Raj Kumar Sharda (office bearers of the Indian Cultural and Welfare Society) with Mr Hamblet Cresswell, Coventry's first Lord Mayor, and Sohrab Modi.

IV   Appendices

I am standing on the left at a meeting of the ICWS. The speaker is welcoming our president and the Assistant High Commissioner of India.

The President, Mr Cresswell, first Lord Mayor of Coventry is replying.

IV   Appendices

Appendix 3: The Hindu Temple Society (Coventry)

The (former) Hindu Temple, Coventry, 274 Stoney Stanton Road. I am talking to my friend, Mr Ravinder Judge.

Outside the (former) Hindu Temple in Coventry. A *murti* (image of deity) is about to be ceremonially installed. I am standing on a lorry with members of the family who had donated the image of the goddess, Ambe Mata. They are performing *arati* (a way of worshipping that involves circling a little light, on a steel tray in front of the deity). In one of her hands the Goddess holds a sword, and I am just behind. Far left: Mr Janak Raj Chibba.

I am sitting inside the (former) Hindu Temple between my friends, Mr Banwari Lal Sharma and Mr Ravinder Judge, 1990.

During construction of the present Hindu Temple, 380 Stoney Stanton Road, Coventry, we had to wear hard hats and high visibility jackets. From left to right: Kiran Garg, me, Kant Kumar Bansal, Jatinder Sharma.

IV Appendices

The sign outside the present Hindu Temple, Coventry.

The present Hindu Temple, Coventry.

The deities in the Hindu Temple as they appeared soon after their ceremonial installation (*murti pratishta*) in January 2012.

The deities in 2015: Far left is Balaji (also known as Venkateshvara) who is mainly worshipped by Hindus from South India. Beside him (to the right in red) are Krishna and his consort Radha. The central group of three figures in yellow consists of Rama, flanked by his brother Lakshman (like Rama, carrying a bow) and Sita, Rama's wife. The two figures dressed in green are Vishnu and Lakshmi. On the far right is the Goddess, Mataji, whose many names include Sheranwali Ma (literally the Mother on a lion or tiger).

IV   Appendices

Two trustees and two committee members holding a *chunni* (donated cloth) which Panditji (the priest) will drape over the *murti* of the Goddess. From left to right: Pavan Kumar, Tarsem Lal, Jatinder Sharma, P.K. Bhakri and me.

The temple dining room. Meals (always vegetarian) are served here whenever there is a special function in the temple.

Lunch on the day that Professor Sato visited our temple in 2013.

I am sitting beside Mr Ram Piara Farmah, chairman of the trustees.

IV   Appendices

Jatinder Sharma (vice president of the Hindu Temple) and I.

My 'lifetime achievement award' presented to me by the Hindu Temple in 2014. (nos. 5–8, 10–11, 14–15: photos by the editor)

Same as fig. 14.

IV Appendices

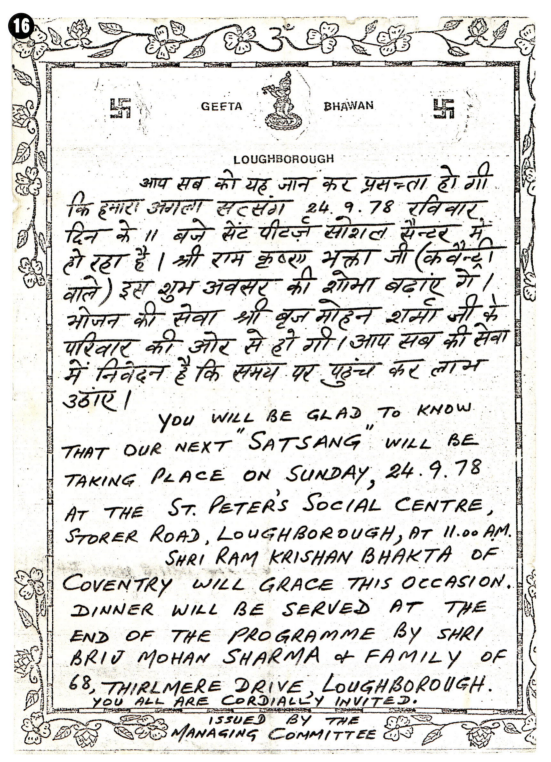

Publicity for one of my visits to Loughborough as the principal speaker in 1978. (Bhakta means devotee.)

IV Appendices

The Aylesford School

From 1988, one of the many letters of appreciation that I have received after speaking to pupils.

IV   Appendices

The Master of the Household
has received Her Majesty's command to invite

Mr. Ram Krishan Prashar

to a Reception to be given at Buckingham Palace
by The Queen and The Duke of Edinburgh
for representatives of different faiths
on Monday, 10th June 2002, at 6.00 p.m.

A reply is requested to:
The Master of the Household,   *Dress: Lounge Suit/Day Dress*
Buckingham Palace,   *or equivalent*
London SW1A 1AA.

Guests are asked to arrive between 5.20 and 5.50 p.m.

I have been invited to some wonderful events as a Hindu representative. One was at Buckingham Palace in 2002.

IV Appendices

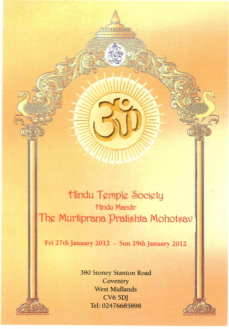
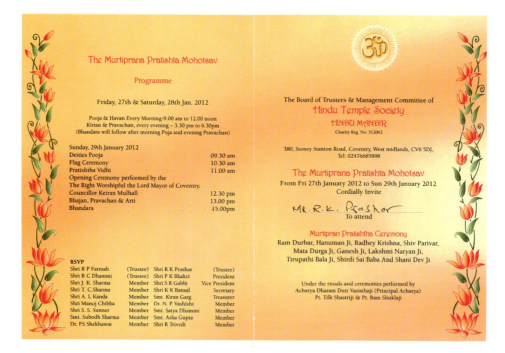

On 27th–29th January 2012 the images of the deities were ceremonially installed in the present temple. Here is my invitation to the 'murtiprana pratishta mohotsav'.

One of the countless letters that schoolchildren have sent me after school visits to the Hindu Temple.

IV Appendices

Appendix 4: Coventry Multi-Faith Forum

Membership Form

Name ....
Address..
....
....
....
Telephone number/Email ....
....
Religious tradition ....

I wish to become a member of Coventry Multi-Faith Forum. I support the aims and objectives of Coventry Multi-Faith Forum outlined in this leaflet.
I enclose the sum of £3.00 as membership fee.

Signed ....

Please send to the Treasurer:
Mr. Kant Kumar Bansal
36 Asthill Grove, Styvechale,
Coventry CV3 6HP

TRUSTEES

Role	Name	Tradition
Chairperson	Miss Veena Dhamu	(Sikh)
Vice Chairperson	Mr. Osman Sheikh	(Muslim)
Secretary	Revd Supriyo Mukherjee	(Christian)
Assistant Secretary	Miss Mehru Fitter	(Zoroastrian)
Treasurer	Mr. Kant Kumar Bansal	(Arya Samaj)
Trustee	Dr. Sara Kalvala	(Buddhist)
Trustee	Mr. Babu Garala	(Hindu)
Trustee	Mr. Ram Krishan	(Hindu)
Trustee	Mr. Harry Hall	(West Indian)
Trustee	Pru Porretta	(Christian)

COVENTRY MULTI-FAITH FORUM

Multi-Faith Centre, Priory Row,
Coventry CV1 5EX.
Company No. 3861480

Coventry Multi-Faith Forum

Coventry Multi-Faith Forum is a charitable initiative representing people from all the major faith traditions found in and around Coventry. The Forum came into existence in 1996.

Membership of the Forum consists of individuals from Arya Samaj, Bahai, Buddhist, Christian, Hindu, Muslim, Sikh, West Indian and Zoroastrian communities.

The aim of the Forum is to celebrate diversity and foster harmony between different communities by increasing knowledge and understanding of each other's ideals. At an individual level the Forum endeavours to encourage personal development through promoting higher values in our daily lives.

Our activities are wide ranging and include addressing issues which affect all communities, such as the teaching of mother-tongue languages, discussing questions of identity faced by young people, religious education and racism. We also take part in positive activities such as the 'Peace Walk' and 'One-World Week' celebrations.

The Multi-Faith Forum can also act as a channel of communication to voice concerns and aspirations of minority communities on any matters of local or national importance.

On 8th June 2002, the Forum took over management of a Multi-Faith Centre in the heart of the City, providing a focal point for hosting multi-faith events, such as displays, celebrations and discussion evenings.

The Multi-faith Centre is part of the City Council's Phoenix Initiative Millennium Building and has come about through collaboration between the Forum and the City Council.

For more information about our activities, please speak to any Trustee listed overleaf or contact the Secretary:

Revd Supriyo Mukherjee,
16 Nunts Lane, Coventry CV6 4HB
E-mail: Samukh@lineone.net
Telephone. 024 7636 3064

Membership

Anyone living in Coventry or the surrounding area, who belongs to a recognised faith group and is sympathetic to our aims, is eligible to join the Multi-Faith Forum.

Membership fees currently stand at £3.00 a year.

Please fill in the membership application form overleaf and you will receive a receipt, and your name will be added to our mailing list for information about activities during the year. As a member, you will be able to vote at the AGM.

Introduction to Coventry Multi-Faith Forum

IV Appendices

'Peace walk with Lady Godiva': The Coventry Multi-Faith Forum's annual Peace Walk (*Coventry Telegraph*). Pru Poretta is locally well-known. Dressed as Lady Godiva, our 11th century landowner and champion of the poor, Pru serves the community tirelessly. The Revd Supriyo Mukherjee helped found the Coventry Multi-Faith Forum.

The Coventry Multi-Faith Forum's annual Peace Walk setting off from Priory Row, Coventry. I am walking with fellow trustees.

IV   Appendices

The Coventry Multi-Faith Forum's Peace Walk, going past the excavated site of the former priory.

The walkers pausing near the ruins of the old cathedral.

Me in Coventry city centre with a local Muslim, Hindu and Sikh.

IV   Appendices

Me standing near the Jain symbol in the Multi-Faith Forum, 2015. (nos. 7–13: photos by the editor)

The display of various faiths in the Multi-Faith Forum, 2015.

The display of Sikhism, Hinduism, Zoroastrianism and other faiths.

Symbols of world religions, 2015.

111

IV   Appendices

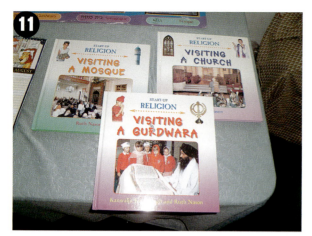

Start Up Religion' books (*Visiting a Mosque, Visiting a Gurdwara, Visiting a Church*), 2015.

True Meaning of Peace, 2015.

Harry Hall, the chairman of the Multi-Faith Forum, with me, 2015.

IV   Appendices

Hiroshima Day service on Saturday 6th August 2016 in Coventry Cathedral (photo by Mr Mike Lane).

Eleanor and me with Mr Harry Hall, Chair of the Multi-Faith Forum, after the annual Hiroshima Day service in 2016 (photo by Mr Mike Lane).

IV   Appendices

A brief history of Coventry Multi-Faith Forum

In the last two decades of the 20th Century, monthly meetings of Coventry Inter Faith group were held at the Franciscan Convent, 63 Blackwell Road. These were attended by representatives of different faiths, who were interested in thematic discussions.

The group received a huge boost with the appointment of Revd. Supriyo Mukherjee as Diocesan Community Relations Adviser and Team Vicar, St. Barnabas. He drew together people from diverse faiths and ensured that a new body with a constitution was formed. Coventry Multi-Faith Forum came into existence in 1996, with meetings taking place at the residence of Revd. Supriyo Mukherjee. Coventry Multi-Faith Forum was registered with Companies House as a charitable initiative (Company No. 3861480).

In the late 90s a former bishop of Coventry, the Rt. Revd. Simon Barrington-Ward, started informal meetings of representatives of different faiths, and expressed an interest in seeing the multi-faith dimension of Coventry reflected in the Phoenix Millennium Initiative, which would help to regenerate the city centre.

This led to lots of meetings, correspondence and liaison with a number of individuals and organisations. Revd. Mukherjee liaised with: John Hayward, Humanities Adviser in Education [and] John McGuigan, Director, City Development. At meetings, the Forum was represented by Revd. Mukherjee, Sheikh Osman, Mike Regan, Babu Garala, Ram Krishan and Mehru Fitter.

A draft proposal for the setting up of a multi-faith centre as part of the bid for the Heritage Quarter was submitted on 6th August 1996.

On 26th February 1998 we received the welcome news that Coventry had succeeded in obtaining the Millennium Grant.

At a well-attended meeting held at the Muslim Resource Centre on 2nd September, diverse faith communities unanimously approved of a multi-faith facility, which would be called Coventry Multi-Faith Centre.

The combined efforts of the Bishop, Revd. Supriyo Mukherjee and Trustees of Coventry Multi-Faith Forum and the assistance of Chris Beck, the Director of Phoenix Initiative, resulted in the upper level of Priory Visitor Centre in becoming the home of Coventry Multi-Faith Forum. We made sure that our Forum was registered with the Companies House as a charitable company.

The Forum took over management of Coventry Multi-Faith Centre on 8th June 2002.

Right from its inception, the Forum has maintained close links with Coventry City

Council and participated in corporate events such as Heritage Open Days, Peace Festival, Inter Faith Week, etc. Also the Forum is represented at Inter Faith and Community meetings held by Coventry City Council.

A major challenge for the Forum has been finding sources of funding. Our success in 3 major funding applications enabled us to buy book and non-book resources, display boards, a computer, some furniture and also to set up our website.

Trustees and members have continued to pay their membership fees and have also made generous donations.

We continue to hold monthly meetings, which are sometimes attended by visitors.

Visiting groups have included students, German visitors to the city, university chaplains attending an international conference at Coventry University, etc.

Mehru Fitter 2015

IV Appendices

A New Year Declaration of Faith Leaders in Coventry

As leaders of different faith communities in Coventry we met last week to share our concerns about the possible war in Iraq. We are completely united in the following matters:

- We do not believe that such a war would be morally justified. According to our faith traditions, an unprovoked attack on Iraq would be contrary to our belief in the right to life and dignity of all.

- We fear that, despite assertions to the contrary, military action would be seen by many as an attack on Islam. This would undermine the considerable trust that currently exists between our various religious communities and could all too easily provoke a violent backlash.

- We call upon our political leaders to continue working for peace through diplomatic means, particularly by honouring the work of the UN weapons inspectors.

- We believe that peace in the Middle East cannot be separated from the search for justice in Israel/Palestine and in other places of conflict.

- We delight in our common inheritance in God and in the richness of our faith traditions. We value the contribution made by the many ethnic and faith groups to the community life of this city.

- We pledge ourselves to live together as good neighbours, building social inclusion, respecting the integrity of each other's religious and cultural inheritance.

- We commit ourselves to any joint action that might promote peace and guard against violence.

Signed: Mamood Anwar, Bishop of Coventry, Gula Chaudahary, Ram Krishan, Osmand Sheikh, Balbir Singh, Christopher Lamb and Tim Brooke

10th January 2003

'A New Year Declaration of Faith Leaders in Coventry' (January 2003) expressing our commitment to peace, as war in Iraq became more likely.

Coventry Evening Telegraph October 25, 2005

150 join annual walk for peace

More than 150 people turned out for an annual peace walk in Coventry city centre. The event, organised by the Multi-Faith Forum as part of Coventry Peace Month, visited Christian, Muslim, Hindu and Sikh places of worship as well as the Multi-Faith Centre in Priory Row.

It finished at Gurdwara Sikh Temple in Harnall Lane at midday with a free meal for all participants. Co-chair of the Multi-Faith Forum, Mehru Fitter, said she thought Saturday's event was the best attended in the history of the walks.

She said: "We have had a fantastic turnout. It broadened everyone's horizons and we all learned the lesson that there is unity in diversity."

Economics and politics student Joe Howlett, aged 20, from Warwick University, arrived with 10 other members of the United World College Society.

He said they were among the youngest present and added: "It was good to have a mixture of ages and cultures. It was a fabulous day out. As students we don't often escape the bubble of Warwick University so to experience the religious and cultural aspects of the city was really interesting."

Coventry Peace Month runs until November 15.

IV Appendices

Appendix 5: Other activities of Mr Ram Krishan

Enjoying my garden in Coventry c. 2012.

Same as fig. 1.

Our black and white cat, Shaitan, a popular member of the family (1980–1997).

Our ginger cat, Billa, who spent seven years with us (1998–2005).

IV   Appendices

'Everybody needs good neighbours'. None could be better than the Gohil family. This is Kamlesh Gohil's fiftieth birthday.

Kamlesh Gohil's fiftieth birthday party.

I have spent many happy hours in Coventry's libraries, reading and meeting my friends. Here I am in discussion in Foleshill Library.

I love reading – especially Hindi literature.

IV   Appendices

With a famous Hindi novelist, Ganga Prasad Vimal (centre) and a fine Hindi poet and story writer, Pran Sharma (far right) at one of Coventry's libraries: Pran Sharma and I spend many hours on the phone discussing Hindi literature.

Me at a *mushaira*, an Urdu poetry conference, in Coventry.

In Stratford-upon-Avon, Warwickshire, with Hindi writers from the UK and India. Left to right: me, Dr K. K. Srivastava, Titiksha Shah, Shailendra Agarwal, Pran Sharma, Usha Mahajan (a famous writer from India).

IV   Appendices

I am often called on to make a speech, especially at Hindu events and in multi-faith meetings.

I have maintained my interest in Sanskrit. Here, with my late friend, John Linton, I am reading the Sanskrit inscription in the entrance of the Old Indian Institute Building in Oxford. John Linton spent some years in India and founded the Quaker Universalist Group.

IV   Appendices

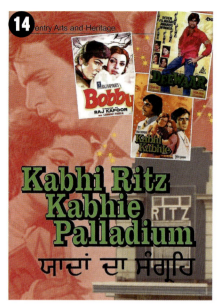 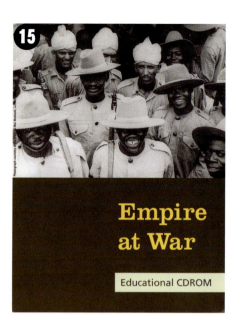

I contributed to an exhibition at the Herbert Museum and Art Gallery, Coventry on Asian cinema in the city: 'Kabhi Ritz Kabhi Palladium'. This title refers to a popular film *Kabhi Khushi Kabhie Gam* and to the names of two local rival cinemas where Bollywood movies were shown.

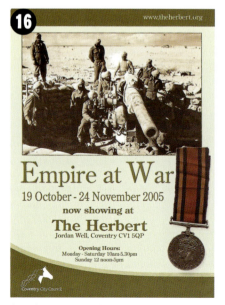 

Another project that I took part in was 'Empire at War' and I spoke about my memories of being in Calcutta and Punjab during World War II.

THE RT HON TONY McNULTY MP
HARROW EAST

HOUSE OF COMMONS
LONDON SW1A 0AA

Mr Ram Krishan Prasher
National Council of Hindu Temples
67 Ulverscroft Road
Cheylesmore Coventry
CV3 5EY

Dear Mr Ram Krishan Prasher,

I am delighted to have received the nomination form from your organisation to attend the celebration of Ramnavami at the House of Commons on 23rd April 2008 organised by myself and Abhay Lakhani (Parliamentary Advisor on Community issues) and supported by National Council of Hindu Temples, Hindu Academy, Pardesh Weekly and Khubi.com.

I personally wanted to thank you for taking the time to be part of this historic event which I believe will be the largest single gathering of Hindu Organisations under One roof in the United Kingdom. I understand the incredible call upon your time but would like to extend our appreciation in the positive response and sincerely hope that you will participate in this momentous event.

Date: Wednesday 23rd April 2008
Time: 3.00 pm to 6.00 pm.
Venue: Members Dining Room – House of Commons – Westminster

Please find enclosed your invitation card which is non transferable and is numbered for security purposes.

The event in the Members Dining room is strictly timed for 4.00 pm to 6.00 pm. The entrance to the House of Commons is via St Stephens's gate. The revised security procedures are strict and we suggest that members attend at 3.00 pm and it will enable us to meet and network for an hour before the event. We will all be meeting at 3.00 pm in Westminster Hall where the media covering the event will also be present.

It would be advisable to use London Transport as parking is restricted, the nearest tube station is Westminster.

I look forward to seeing you at this historic event in the House of Commons.

Yours Sincerely

Tony McNulty

The celebration of Ramnavami at the House of Commons in 2008.

IV   Appendices

Westminster, 2008.

I enjoy attending the Annual Meeting of Coventry Council in Coventry Cathedral. Here I am with the new Lord Mayor in 2009.

It was a privilege to meet Sir Richard Attenborough, director of the film *Gandhi*, at South Africa House, London.

I was delighted to meet Sir Mark Tully, distinguished writer and broadcaster, in the Divinity School in Cambridge during a Dharam Hinduja Institute for Indic Research conference.

IV   Appendices

I love travelling. I have tried a camel (Port El Kantaoui, Tunisia).

A Javanese rickshaw (Jogyakarta, Indonesia) on Christmas Day 1991.

A narrow gauge train in West Wales. Some modes of transport are more comfortable than others.

I went up in a hot air balloon and saw the sun rise over the Valley of the Kings in Egypt. Landing in a field of sugarcane reminded me of Punjab. (In Hindi one word for sugar '*misri*' means 'Egyptian'.)

IV   Appendices

Eleanor and I spent a month in Indonesia in 1991. I had known for many years about Bali's Hindu culture and Bali is the place I most want to revisit. Here I am with Eleanor at the royal palace in Ubud.

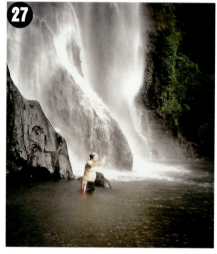

In north Bali I bathed in the Singsing waterfall.

Tirta Gangga water palace in east Bali.

In December 1993 Eleanor and I travelled to Rameshvaram in Tamil Nadu where I performed a ceremony for my deceased parents. Here is Eleanor's poem about this:

SHRADDH - A POEM

'A good day - Kartika - full moon'.
A temple guide, hopeful of custom,
Greets us by the train, hears us explain
That we have come for Shraddh, come to perform
The rites that free the souls of the deceased
From more rebirths. He will, he says, ensure
That all is done aright.

Dwarfed by the temple's towering gopuram -
Tapering stone, alive with sculpted forms -
Pilgrims and vendors, beggars, cattle, crows,
Are one with sea and sky,
One with the ancient sage's certainty
That all is one.

On the beach we sit, the priest
Banded with ashen marks, recites in Sanskrit,
Asking the names of the deceased. He is alert, prepared
With all we need - bananas, garlands, milk,
Coconut, flour, dried grasses
And umbrella, tucked away in case it rains.

Raucous crows, eager attentive goat, mild watchful cow
And you, hung with a Brahmin thread,
Naming your father, mother, kin
Across the generations. Bidden by the priest
You knead the milk and flour to doughy balls.
A crow snaps one, the cow receives the rest.
The waves accept the garlands.
Obediently we give bananas to a cow along the way

Towards the temple, where the guide
Draws water from each sacred well,
Drenches you, guides us through
Pillared avenues to shadowed shrines
Arched by the steady glow of myriad flames,
Arch beyond arch.

Multi - dimensional infinity enwombed;
Space, time, present, past,
Life, death all one
This fulsome moonlit night
Of Kartika.

From Rameshwaram we travelled to our family home in Mohalla Pathakan in Nawanshahr, Punjab. This was the view from our rooftop in December 1993 when we set out on a pilgrimage in the hills.

IV   Appendices

Our first stop was at Chintpurni. This is the marble paved street to the temple.

The entrance to the temple 'Shri Chhinn-Mastika Dham' at Chintpurni.

Puneet and I entering the temple.

Here we are arriving at our next stop, the Jwalaji temple.

Eleanor and Puneet are standing with their offerings in the Jwalaji temple.

IV Appendices

Eleanor and I with the priest in Jwalaji in 1993. In the temple you can see flames coming out of the ground (as it is a volcanic area). We regard these as showing the presence of the Goddess.

This commemorates the visit of the Mughal emperor Akbar to this sacred place.

A shrine in the temple at Kangra in 1993.

Dawn in Chamunda in 1993.

Eleanor, Puneet and I in the temple at Kangra, in 1993.

IV   Appendices

Some of my many Coventry friends

Mr Ravinder Judge with me.

Mr Banwari Lal Sharma with me.

Here I am in Coventry city centre with my friends Ali Sahib (centre) and Iqbal Sahib (left). We meet each weekday for tea and we often discuss Indian and Pakistani politics and religion.

IV Appendices

Appendix 6: Ethnicity and religion in the UK and Coventry

Table 1 Ethnicity in the UK and Coventry (2001 Census)

Ethnic Group	UK Population	%	Coventry Population	%
White	54,153,898	92.1	252,643	83.98
British	50,366,497	85.67	235,632	78.32
Irish	691,232	1.2	10,401	3.46
Other White	3,096,169	5.27	6,610	2.2
Mixed	677,117	1.2	5,163	1.72
White & Black Caribbean	—	—	2,453	0.82
White & Black African	—	—	271	0.09
White & Asian	—	—	1,605	0.53
Other Mixed	—	—	834	0.28
Asian or Asian British	2,331,423	4.0	33,910	11.27
Indian	1,053,411	1.8	24,177	8.03
Pakistani	747,285	1.3	6,169	2.05
Bangladeshi	283,063	0.5	1,741	0.58
Other Asian	247,664	0.4	1,823	0.61
Black or Black British	1,148,738	2.0	5,412	1.8
Caribbean	565,876	1.0	3,314	1.1
African	485,277	0.8	1,679	0.56
Other Black	97,585	0.2	419	0.14
Chinese	247,403	0.4	2,183	0.73
Other Ethnic Group	230,615	0.4	1,537	0.51
Total	58,789,194	100	300,848	100.0

Table 2 Religion in the UK and Coventry (2001 Census)

Religion	UK Population	%	Coventry Population	%
Christian	42,079,000	71.6	196,346	65.26
Buddhist	152,000	0.3	784	0.26
Hindu	559,000	1.0	7,757	2.58
Jewish	267,000	0.5	222	0.07
Muslim	1,591,000	2.7	11,686	3.88
Sikh	336,000	0.6	13,960	4.64
Other religion	179,000	0.3	733	0.24
No religion	9,104,000	15.5	45,314	15.06
Religion not stated	4,289,000	7.3	24,046	8.0
Base	58,789,000	100	300,848	100.0

IV   Appendices

[2011 Census]

Table 1 Ethnicity in the UK and Coventry (2011 Census)

Ethnic Group	UK		Coventry	
	Population	%	Population	%
White	55,010,359	87.07	234,029	73.84
English/Welsh/Scottish/Northern Irish/British	———	———	211,188	66.63
Irish	———	———	7,305	2.3
Gypsy or Irish Traveller	63,193	0.1	151	0.05
Other White			15,385	4.85
Mixed/Multiple Ethnic Groups	1,250,229	1.98	8,190	2.58
White & Black Caribbean	———	———	3,672	1.16
White & Black African	———	———	943	0.3
White & Asian	———	———	2,388	0.75
Other Mixed	———	———	1,227	0.39
Asian/Asian British	4,373,339	6.92	51,598	16.28
Indian	1,451,862	2.3	27,751	8.76
Pakistani	1,174,983	1.86	9,510	3.0
Bangladeshi	451,529	0.71	2,951	0.93
Chinese	433,150	0.69	3,728	1.18
Other Asian	861,815	1.36	7,658	2.42
Black	1,904,684	3.01	17,764	5.6
African	———	———	12,836	4.05
Caribbean	———	———	3,317	1.05
Other Black	———	———	1,611	0.51
Other Ethnic Group	580,374	0.92	5,339	1.68
Arab	240,240	0.38	2,020	0.64
Any Other Ethnic Group	340408	0.54	3,319	1.05
Total	63,182,178	100.0	316,960	100.0

Table 2 Religion in the UK and Coventry (2011 Census)

Religion	UK		Coventry	
	Population	%	Population	%
Christian	37,583,962	59.49	170,090	53.66
Buddhist	261,584	0.41	1,067	0.34
Hindu	835,394	1.3	11,152	3.52
Jewish	269,568	0.43	210	0.07
Muslim	2,786,635	4.41	23,665	7.47
Sikh	432,429	0.68	15,912	5.02
Other religion	262,774	0.42	1,641	0.52
No religion	16,221,509	25.67	72,896	23.0
Religion not stated	4,528,323	7.17	20,327	6.41
Total	63,182,178	100.0	316,960	100.0

IV Appendices

Appendix 7: Maps of the Punjab region (India) and of Coventry in the UK

1 The Sub-Continent of India and location of Punjab

IV Appendices

2 Partition of Punjab, 1947

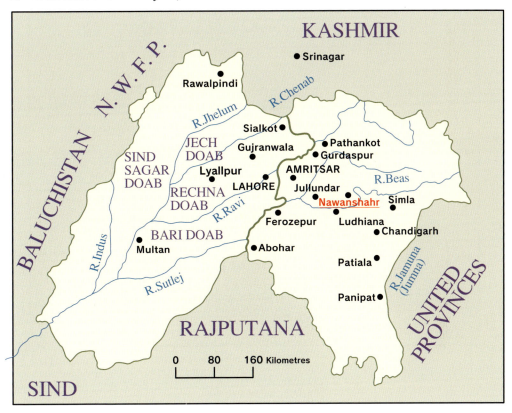

IV Appendices

3 Punjab after reorganisation in 1966

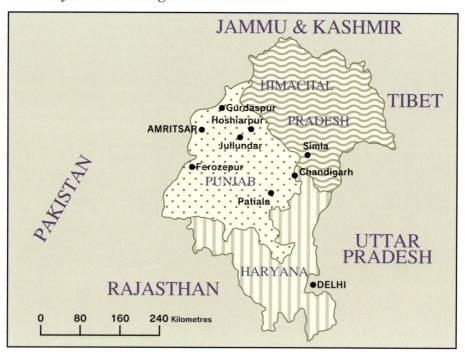

IV   Appendices

4   Present Punjab state of India

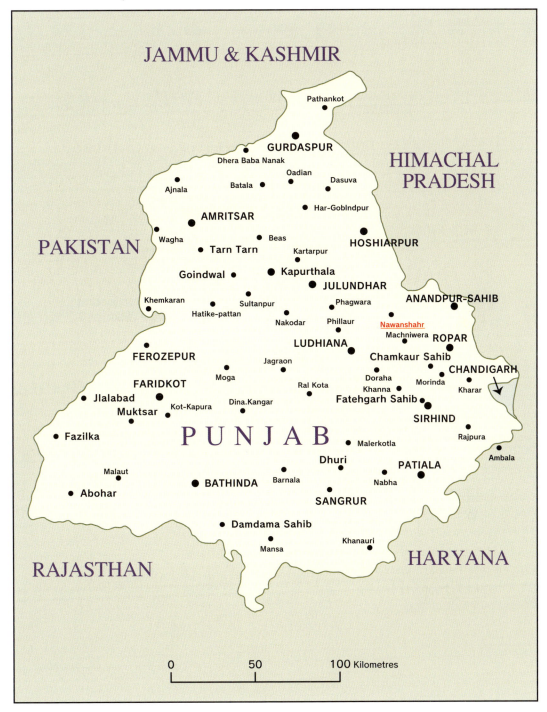

IV Appendices

5 Coventry

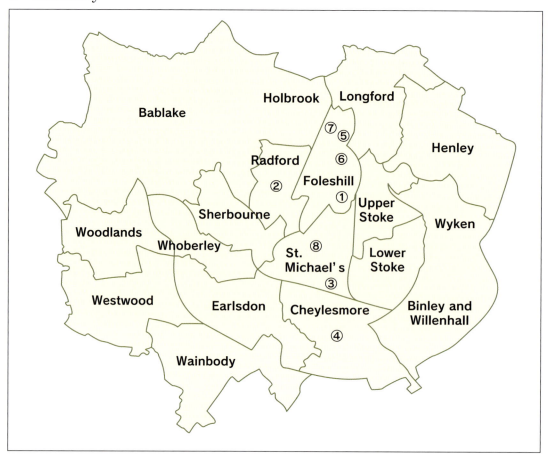

① Princess Street
② Wyley Road
③ St Patrick's Road
④ Ulverscroft Road
⑤ Alfred Herbert Limited
⑥ The Hindu Temple Society (Coventry)
⑦ The Indian Community Centre
⑧ The Multi-Faith Forum

Appendix 8: Select bibliography and websites

Hindu tradition

- Clothey, Fred W., *Religion in India: A Historical Introduction,* London & New York: Routledge, 2006.
- Johnson, W. J., *Oxford Dictionary of Hinduism*, Oxford: Oxford University Press, 2009.
- Kanitkar, V.P. & Cole, W. Owen (eds), *Hinduism*, Abingdon: Bookprint, 1995 (2010).
- Klostermaier, Klaus K., *A Concise Encyclopedia of Hinduism*, Oxford: Oneworld, 1998 (2003).
- Klostermaier, Klaus K., *Hinduism: A Short History*, Oxford: Oneworld, 2000.
- Knott, Kim, *Hinduism A Very Short Introduction*, Oxford: Oxford University Press, 1998 (2016 second edition).
- Rodrigues, P. Hillary, *Introducing Hinduism*, New York: Routledge, 2006.
- Sen, K. M., *Hinduism*, Harmondsworth: Penguin Books, 1961.
- Seshagiri, Rao, K. L. (chief ed.), *Encyclopedia of Hinduism*, 11 vols., Mandala Pub., 2013.
- Zaehner, R. C., *Hinduism*, London: Oxford University Press, 1962.

Life in Punjab and historical events in India mentioned in this book

- Brass, Paul R., *Language, Religion and Politics in North India*, Cambridge: Cambridge University Press, 1974 (2005).
- Brown, Judith (ed.), *The Essential Works of Mahatma Gandhi*, Oxford: Oxford University Press, 2007.
- Campbell-Johnson, Alan, *Mission with Mountbatten*, London: Robert Hale, 1952.
- Collins, Larry & Lapierre, Dominique, *Freedom at Midnight*, HarperCollins, 1975.
- Khan, Yasmin, *The Great Partition: The Making of India and Pakistan*, New Haven: Yale University Press, 2008.
- Khan, Yasmin, *India at War: The Subcontinent and the Second World War*, Oxford: Oxford University Press, 2015.
- Mir, Farina, *The Social Space of Language: Vernacular Culture in British Colonial Punjab*, Berkeley: University of California Press, 2010.
- Narain, Savita, *The Historiography of the Jallianwala Bagh Massacre, 1919*, Surrey: Spantech & Lancer, 1998.
- Panayi, Panikos & Virdee, Pippa (eds), *Refugees and the End of Empire: Imperial Collapse and Forced Migration during the Twentieth Century*, Basingstoke: Palgrave Macmillan, 2011.
- Talbot, Ian (ed.), *The Independence of India and Pakistan: New Approaches and Reflections*, Oxford: Oxford University Press, 2013.
- Talbot, Ian & Singh, Gurharpal, *The Partition of India*, Cambridge: Cambridge University Press, 2009.
- Zamindar, Vazira Fazila-Yacoobali, *The Long Partition and the Making of Modern South Asia: Refugees, Boundaries, Histories*, New York: Columbia University Press, 2007 (Paperback edition, 2010).

IV   Appendices

Hindus and South Asians more generally in the UK

- Lal, Brij V. (ed.), *The Encyclopedia of the Indian Diaspora*, Honolulu: University of Hawai'i Press, 2006.
- Zavos, John, Kanungo, Pralay, Reddy, Deepa S., Warrier, Maya & Williams, Raymond Brady (eds), *Public Hinduisms*, London: Sage, 2012.
- Ali, N., Kalra, V. S. & Sayyid, S. (eds), *A Postcolonial People: South Asians in Britain*, London: Hurst & Company, 2006.
- Ballard, R. (ed.), *Desh Pardesh: The South Asian Presence in Britain*, London: Hurst & Company, 1994 (2006).
- Baumann, Gerd, *Contesting Culture: Discourses of Identity in Multi-Ethnic London*, Cambridge: Cambridge University Press, 1996.
- Bowen, D. (ed.), *Hinduism in England*, Bradford: Bradford College, 1981.
- Brown, Callum G., *Religion and Society in Twentieth-Century Britain*, MacHarlow: Pearson Longman, 2006.
- Brown, Judith. & Foot, Rosemary (eds), *Migration: The Asian Experience*, Basingstoke: Macmillan, 1994.
- Burghart R. (ed.), *Hinduism in Great Britain: The Perpetuation of Religion in an Alien Cultural Milieu*, London: Tavistock, 1987.
- Coward, Harold, Hinnells, John R. & Williams, Raymond Brady (eds), *The South Asian Religious Diaspora in Britain, Canada, and the United States*, New York: State University of New York Press, 2000.
- Desai, R., *Indian Immigrants in Britain*, London: Oxford University Press, 1963.
- Fisher, Michael H, Lahiri, Shompa & Thandi, Shinder (eds), *A South-Asian History of Britain: Four Centuries of Peoples from the Indian Sub-Continent*, Oxford: Greenwood World Publishing, 2007.
- Haar, G. ter (ed.), *Strangers and Sojourners: Religious Communities in Diaspora*, Leuven: Peeters, 1998.
- Heath, Deana & Mathur, Chandana (eds), *Communalism and Globalization in South Asia and its Diaspora*, London: Routledge, 2011.
- Jackson. Robert & Nesbitt, Eleanor, *Listening to Hindus*, London: Unwin Hyman, 1990.
- Jackson, Robert & Nesbitt, Eleanor, *Hindu Children in Britain*, Stoke-on-Trent: Trentham Book, 1993.
- Kanitkar, H. & Jackson, R., *Hindus in Britain*, London: University of London (SOAS), 1982.
- Knott, Kim, *Hinduism in Leeds: A Study of Religious Practices in the Indian Hindu Community and in Hindu-Related Groups*, Leeds: Community Religions Project at the University of Leeds, 1986.
- Lipner, Julius, *Hindus: Their Religious Beliefs and Practices*, London: Routledge, 1994.
- Nasta, Susheila (ed.), *India in Britain: South Asian Networks and Connections, 1858–1950*, Basingstoke: Palgrave Macmillan, 2013.
- Nesbitt, Eleanor, *Intercultural Education: Ethnographic and Religious Approaches*, Brighton: Sussex Academic Press, 2004.

- Nye, Malory, *A Place for our Gods: The Construction of an Edinburgh Hindu Temple Community*, London: Taylor & Francis, 1995.
- Parsons, Gerald (ed.), *The Growth of Religious Diversity: Britain from 1945, vol.1: Traditions*, London: Routledge, 1993.
- Puri, Kailash & Nesbitt, Eleanor, *Pool of Life: The Autobiography of a Punjabi Agony Aunt*, Eastbourne: Sussex Academic Press, 2013.
- Raj, Dhooleka Sarhadi, *Where are you from? Middle-Class Migrants in the Modern World*, Berkeley: University of California Press, 2003.
- Ranasinha, Ruvani et al. (eds), *South Asians and Shaping of Britain, 1870–1950: A Sourcebook,* Manchester: Manchester University Press, 2012.
- Shukla, Sandhya, *India Abroad: Diasporic Cultures of Postwar America and England*, Princeton: Princeton University Press, 2003.
- Suri, Sanjay, *Brideless in Wembley*, New Delhi: Penguin India, 2006.
- Thomas, Terence (ed.), *The British: Their Religious Beliefs and Practices 1800–1986*, London & New York: Routledge, 1988.
- Visram, Rozina, *Asians in Britain: 400 Years of History*, London: Pluto Press, 2002.
- Visram, Rozina, *The History of the Asian Community in Britain*, London: Hodder Wayland Publisher, 1995.
- Weller, Paul (ed.), *Religions in the UK: Directory 2001–03*, Derby: the Multi-Faith Centre at the University of Derby, 2001.
- Woodhead, Linda & Catto, Rebecca, *Religion and Change in Modern Britain*, London: Routledge, 2012.

Mr Ram Krishan's work and interests: Alfred Herbert's, Bollywood, Indian Workers' Association (IWA) and Interfaith Encounter

- Dudrah, Rajinder, *Bollywood: Sociology Goes to the Movies*, London & New Delhi: Sage Publications, 2008.
- Dudrah, Rajinder Kumar, *Bollywood Travels: Culture, Diaspora and Border Crossings in Popular Hindi Cinema*, London: Routledge, 2012.
- Eck, Diana L., *Encountering God: A Spiritual Journey from Bozeman to Banaras*, Boston: Beacon Press, 2003.
- Jha. K. Subhash, *The Essential Guide to Bollywood*, New Delhi: Roli Books, 2005.
- John, DeWitt, *Indian Workers' Association in Britain*, Oxford; Oxford University Press, 1969.
- King, John, *Three Asian Associations in Britain*, Monographs in Ethnic Relations, No. 8, Centre for Research in Ethnic Relations, University of Warwick, 1994.
- Josephides, Sasha, *Towards a History of the Indian Workers' Association*, Research Paper in Ethnic Relations, No. 18, Centre for Research in Ethnic Relations, University of Warwick, 1991.
- Klostermeier, Klaus, *Hindu and Christian in Vrindaban*, London: SCM Press, 1969.
- Nesbitt, Eleanor, *Interfaith Pilgrims: Living Truths and Truthful Living*, London: Quaker Books, 2003.
- Lloyd-Jones, Roger & Lewis, Myrddin John, *Alfred Herbert and the British Machine*

IV Appendices

    Tool Industry, 1887–1983, Farnham: Ashgate, 2006.
- Race, Alan, *Interfaith Encounter: The Twin Tracks of Theology and Dialogue*, London: SCM Press, 2001.
- Roy, Anjali Gera & Huat, Chua Beng, *Travels of Bollywood Cinema: From Bombay to LA*, New York: Oxford University Press, 2015.
- Wingate, Andrew, *The Meeting of Opposites? Hindus and Christians in the West*, London: SPCK, 2014.

History of Coventry

[Books and articles]
- Cameron, Jacqueline, *Coventry: Through Time*, Stroud: Amberley Publishing, 2010.
- Donoghue, Daniel, *Lady Godiva: A Literary History of the Legend,* Malden: Blackwell Pub, 2003.
- Doubleday, Herbert Arthur *et al* (eds), *The Victoria History of the County of Warwick*, vol. 8 (The City of Coventry and Borough of Warwick), London: OUP, 1969.
- Douglas, Alton, Moore, Dennis & Douglas, Jo, *Coventry: A Century of News (A Pictorial Record)*, Brewin Books Ltd, 1991 (2011).
- Fox, Levi, *Coventry's Heritage*, Coventry: Coventry Evening Telegraph, 1957.
- French, K. L, 'The Legend of Lady Godiva and the Image of the Female Body', *Journal of Medieval History*, 18, 1992, pp. 3–19.
- Lancaster, Bill & Mason, Tony (eds), *Life & Labour in a 20th Century City*, Coventry: Cryfield Press, 1986.
- Lancaster, Joan Cadogan, *Godiva of Coventry*, Coventry: Coventry Corporation, 1967.
- McGrory, David, *Coventry: History and Guide*, Stroud: Alan Sutton, 1993.
- McGrory, David, *The City of Coventry, Images from the Past*, Upton: Jones-Sands, 1996.
- McGrory, David, *Coventry at War*, Stroud: The History Press, 1997.
- McGrory, David, *A History of Coventry*, Chichester: Phillimore, 2003.
- McGrory, David, *The Illustrated History of Coventry's Suburbs*, Goring-By-Sea: Breedon Books, 2003.
- McGrory, David, *Secret Coventry*, Stroud: Amberley Publishing, 2015.
- Nesbitt, Eleanor, *Coventry's Literary Trail*, Coventry, Positive Images Festival, 2014.
- Newbold, E.B, *Portrait of Coventry*, London: Robert Hale Limited, 1972 (1982).
- Richardson, Kenneth, *Twentieth-Century Coventry*, London: The Macmillan Press, 1972.
- Smith, Adrian, *The City of Coventry: A Twentieth Century Icon*, London: I. B. Tauris, 2006.
- Smith, Albert & Fry, David, *The Coventry We Have Lost*, vol. 1, Berkwell: Simanda Press, 1991.
- Smith, Albert & Fry, David, *The Coventry We Have Lost*, vol. 2, Berkwell: Simanda Press, 1993.
- Smith, Frederick, *Six Hundred Years of Municipal Life*, Coventry: The Corporation of the City of Coventry, 1945.
- Soden, Iain, *Coventry: The Hidden History*, Stroud: The History Press, 2013.
- Thoms, David & Donnelly, Tom, *Coventry's Industrial Economy 1880–1980*, Coventry: Cryfield Press.

IV   Appendices

◯ Virdee, Pippa, *Coming to Coventry: Stories from the South Asian Pioneers*, Coventry: Coventry Teaching PCT & The Herbert, 2006.
◯ Walters, Peter, *The Story of Coventry*, Stroud: The History Press, 2013.
◯ Well, Jordan, *Coventry at Work: A Collection of Memories*, Coventry: The Herbert Art Gallery & Museum, 2014.

[Pamphlets, newspapers and others]
◯ *Coventry Evening Telegraph*, October 25, 2005.

Websites

[General]
◯ Spiritual Care – University Hospitals Coventry
  (www.uhcw.nhs.uk/for-patients- and-visitors/spiritual-care)
◯ Heathrow prayer rooms and chapel
  (http://www.heathrow.com/airport-guide/terminal-facilities-and-sevices/prayer-rooms...)
◯ Hiroshima Coventry Club
  (http://www7b.biglobe.ne.jp/~coventryclub)
◯ The Multi-Faith Centre at the University of Derby
  (multi-faithcentre.org)
◯ Sukhmani Sahib Part 1, 2
  (http://www.rajkaregakhalsa.net/sukhmanisahib21.htm;
  http://www.rajkaregakhalsa.net/sukhmanisahib22.htm)

[People]
◯ Bachchan, Harivansh Rai (1907–2003)
  (http://global.britannica.com/biography/Harivansh-Rai-Bachchan)
◯ Bapu, Morari (1946–)
  Ram Katha by Morari Bapu
  (http://www.moraribapu.org/new_2013 moraribapu_biography htmal)
◯ Bhose, Subhash Chandra (1897–1945)
  (http:/www.iloveindia.com/indian-heroes/subhash-chabdra-bose.html)
◯ Gandhi, Mahatma (1869–1948)
  (http://www.history.co.uk/biographies/mahatma-gandhi)
◯ Pritam, Amrita (1919–2005)
  (http://www.poemhunter.com/amirta-pritam/biography/)
◯ Rai, Lala Lajpat (1865–1928)
  (https://global.britannica.com/biography/Lala-Lajpat-Rai)

IV   Appendices

Appendix 9: A message from Mr Ram Krishan

To the readers of this narrative (if there are any) I want to stress this is not autobiography. Some of the things which [I mentioned] during the course of interview with Professor Sato happened a long time ago and [what I said] is based on my memory or what I heard from my parents. So, quite frankly, there could be error in that, although I don't think so. What I am going to stress [is] that all these kinds of errors are my responsibility, not Professor Kiyotaka Sato's, who has very rigorously and patiently interviewed me and recorded the observations and facts as I see it.

I am obliged and honoured that Professor Sato requested me to narrate my life story which is full of happenings – sometimes very strange happenings, which readers might have thought contrary to rational thinking. I very humbly say, about that, that sometimes truth is stranger than fiction. As it happened to me, it is a true statement of my life story.

I am indebted to Professor Sato for all his efforts, patience and perseverance during the course of my interviews, and thanks very much to him for publishing this account of my life story. Thank you as well to Dr Pippa Virdee for her beautiful foreword – it's better than my own narration – my wife, Eleanor Nesbitt, for her valuable suggestions and support throughout the process of producing this booklet. Thank you too to the many individuals who have contributed photographs or whose photographs appear in this booklet.

I hope that what I have said will be of interest to my children and their children.

As I have led my life, I have come to the conclusion, as is expressed in my religious books: *ekam satyam vipra vahudha badanti* [Truth is one, scholars interpret it differently]. My experience in my family and wider society has been multi-faith. We are all children of God and I am reminded also of a great saying in Hinduism: *vasudevo kutumbakam* [The whole world is my family]. My wish is for all the world to live in peace.

Ram Krishan
Coventry
7 January 2016